BELLE TOUT

THE LITTLE LIGHTHOUSE THAT MOVED

Elizabeth Wright

Belle Tout Lighthouse, Beachy Head, Eastbourne, East Sussex. BN20 0AE
English Heritage Building ID293528
OS Grid reference TV 5635695509
OS Grid Coordinates 556356, 95509
Lat/Longitude 50.7381, 0.2145

First published in the UK in September 2013 by MyVoice Publishing

Copyright: © Elizabeth Wright
Elizabeth Wright asserts the moral right to be identified as the author of this work

Published by: MyVoice Publishing Ltd
Unit 1,
16 Maple Road,
Eastbourne,
BN23 6NY

ISBN: 978-1-909359-19-2

Throughout its history Belle Tout has never been far away from excitement, drama and public attention. It's little surprise that visitors to Beachy Head and Eastbourne take a stroll along the cliffs to visit this iconic landmark and take in the panoramic views. One thing that can be said about Belle Tout – the lighthouse is a true survivor.

Stephen Lloyd, MP

Belle Tout at sunset. (Picture by Elizabeth Wright)

FOREWORD

What an epic! This was my first impression of the marvellous, detailed tome produced by Elizabeth.

Belle Tout has always held a fascination for all those who have seen it first hand. Magnificent and filled with story upon story. Elizabeth has captured those stories beautifully and not spared any detail in telling us the enthralling history of this thought provoking edifice.

Well done Elizabeth…a book which will serve as an accurate historical record of one of the best sights in the UK….

Belle Tout…please stay forever…..

DEC CLUSKEY
Owner- The Serious Writers Guild. Dec has been a past King Rat and Trustee of the exclusive show business charity, 'The Grand Order of Water Rats.' Patron and supporter of 'Lark in the Park.' Dec was a founder member of the famous band 'The Bachelors,' which has achieved two number one hits, with 'Diane' and Charmaine;' 18 chart singles; 75 albums; amassed a number of gold and platinum albums. In 2008   they reached the Top Ten in the UK charts with a compilation CD 'I can't believe – the very best of The Bachelors.'

Belle Tout- A summer's evening. (Picture by Elizabeth Wright.)

Contents

PREFACE

I fell in love with Belle Tout lighthouse many years ago. I remember with great affection my very first writing project in 1994 when, as a rookie scribe, I was asked to do a feature article on the sale of this iconic building. As the owner and I sat chatting in the lantern room the sea mist cleared, the sun came out, and the surrounding area was bathed in a breathtakingly surreal golden glow. I wrote with my heart, the article was accepted, and the resultant cheque was most welcome, arriving at a time when I was a penniless single mum bringing up a little girl.

This building is a national treasure. It stands proudly on top of a promontory at Beachy Head, East Sussex, in an area so aptly described by Kipling as 'blunt, bow-headed, whale-backed downs' on whose rolling slopes grow the 'close-bit thyme that smells like dawn in Paradise'. As soon as you step within her boundary walls, Belle Tout's mystique wraps itself around you. The area is timeless, and I was hooked by its magic and enchantment.

I wrote many more articles on Belle Tout, gathering large files of information as I went along. After 20 years I felt that I had enough data, pictures, anecdotes, personal memories and stories to create a book. Further research revealed many more fascinating facts about the lighthouse, so in this book I have attempted to create the definitive record of Belle Tout.

We are so fortunate that the little lighthouse is still on that cliff top. In the 182 years since it was built it has been decommissioned as a working unit (in 1899), shot at and shattered (during the Second World War), abandoned and declared to be a ruin fit only for demolition. It was saved by the decision to give it listed building status in 1949. Caring owners over the years have gently restored Belle Tout, with the grandest gesture being made by the Roberts family, who moved her over 55ft from the crumbling cliff edge, saving her from a watery grave.

Belle Tout looks set to be around for many more years, as the present owner, David Shaw, who bought the lighthouse 'with my heart', has spent nearly a million pounds on restoration, renovation and a new access road, creating a superb and unique bed and breakfast establishment.

Among the dozens of people I interviewed there was one word that came up time and again – happiness. Belle Tout's charisma has a delightful effect on the visitors who pass through her doors.

This book is dedicated to the spirit of Belle Tout.

Elizabeth Wright. Summer 2013

Belle Tout. (Picture by Rob Wassell)

THE SHIPWRECKS

Sussex men that dwell upon the shore

Look out when storms arise and billows roar

Devoutly praying with uplifted hands

That some well-laden ship may strike the sands

To whose rich cargo may they make pretence

And fatten on the spoils of Providence.

William Congreve, 1697

The seas off Beachy Head, in East Sussex, are known locally as the Mariners' Graveyard. The Venetians called it Caput Doble, the Devil's Headland. There are jagged submerged reefs running out from the base of the high chalk cliffs, and, 7 miles into the Channel, the equally hostile rocks of the Royal Sovereign Shoals. Add notorious currents and capricious winds (mostly south-westerlies), and one can understand why there have been so many shipwrecks and deaths in the area. An additional factor was pointed out by a writer in 1834: 'Whether the seamen suffer most from their unskilfulness in navigation or from the incorrectness of their charts, it is uncertain: but most probably from the latter, as all the new charts lay down Beachy Head much farther to sea than the old ones.'

The waters between Rye and Newhaven are located in a narrow section of the English Channel, which accommodates one of the busiest shipping lanes in the world. One of the earliest known recorded disasters here was the shipwreck of the *Marie* of Santander, in 1368.

In 1691 the court of William III and Mary was petitioned by one Thomas Offrey, Lord of the Manor of Birling, for the urgent need of a warning light, 'being sorely troubled by the great numbers of ships and lives lost every year at and near Beachy Head in Sussex. It sheweth that a great number of ships have been heretofore lost and some are lost every year near 'the Beachy' in Sussex being a very dangerous coast in the dark; and whereas nothing is so good to prevent the same loss as a lighthouse.' This plea was referred to Trinity House, Deptford Sound, where it was duly recorded, pigeonholed and forgotten.

With no warning lights there was a continuing succession of devastating shipwrecks off Beachy Head cliffs. On 29 November 1747 the 800 ton *Nympha Americana*, alias *Nuestra Senora De Los Remedios*, a Spanish corsair with 280 persons on board, became separated from an accompanying convoy. The weather was foul, with howling snow-laden winds. As the crew tried desperately to make for the shelter of Pevensey Bay, the ship's underbelly was torn apart on rocks and its superstructure was tossed onto the shore at Birling Gap, breaking up like matchwood. Thirty of the 130 sailors fell into the sea and lost their lives. Commodore George Walker, captain of the *Royal Privateer*, had captured this Spanish-owned 60-gun ship a short time earlier in Cadiz, and was taking it to London. In the hold were gold and silver lace, velvets, clothes, valuable metals, £5,000 in cash, £30,000-worth of quicksilver (mercury used in the refining of gold and silver), brandy, wines and 'almost every other kind of merchandise.' The cargo was insured for £150,000, a lot of money in those days.

As there was a culture in Sussex that any wrecked ship was fair game, word soon got around that a ship was in distress, and crowds of local people came to the beaches, watching like vultures and waiting for the rich pickings. In spite of heavy snow they were ready to plunder the cargo. Those who were well prepared came with horses and wagons, ropes and chains, sacks and boxes. Few attempted to save any of the drowning mariners, and crew and passengers stranded on the beach were cruelly ignored. Corpses were stripped of anything of value. The ship's liquor store was broken into and large casks of brandy were hauled off in carts. Those without transport smashed open the containers and, sitting in the snow, started to drink the contents. About sixty plunderers became so intoxicated that they eventually froze and died where they sat. It is recorded that a woman was found dead with two children weeping by her side. A Mr Richardson from Alciston tumbled to his death from the cliff top.

Horse Guards who were billeted nearby were called in to protect the remains of the cargo, but one soldier couldn't resist the temptation of the gold coins and slipped some into his boots. He was only found out when he was ordered to mount his horse, but couldn't: the weight of the doubloons prevented him from lifting his foot to the stirrup.

The local Controller of Customs, Mr Hurdis, tried to stop the wholesale plundering, but without success. Part owner of the ship, a Mr Bouchier, Member of Parliament for Southwark, heard the disastrous news and, with a warrant from the Secretary of War and aided by a number of soldiers, went to assist Mr Hurdis. Along the way he came face to face with 12 smugglers carrying away their ill-gotten gains. After a stand-off two smugglers were killed and the rest hastily dispersed. A few of the soldiers succumbed to the rick pickings, with four of them being severely whipped at Lewes for stealing goods. Another helped himself to a considerable amount of booty and disappeared.

More goods from the ship were washed ashore during the next few days, as stated in the *Sussex Advertiser:*

'We are informed that during the two or three first days of last week, the goods belonging to the wrecked ship came on shore as thick as they did first, and that there was near as many people on the beach ready to receive them. It is supposed that part of the wreck had lodged upon the rock and was since broken, which set the things contained therein a-floating.

There are fourteen or fifteen of the crew missing. Her lading consists chiefly of bale goods and quicksilver, the latter of which is all sunk in the sands but they are in hopes of recovering it again.'

Another article followed on 4 January 1748: 'There have been two loads of quicksilver brought here [to Lewes] which was weighed up from the bottom of the wrecked ship. We are informed that there is a great quantity lies in deeper water and cannot be got up without a diver, for which reason there is one come down from London who proposes to undertake it by the ton weight.' A few days later the newspaper reported that 'four more loads of quicksilver were brought to Lewes in the last week'. Shortly afterwards some 30 wagonloads were retrieved. Enough of the cargo was salvaged to raise £39,000 when it was auctioned at Lewes. The insurance company paid out £117,000 in compensation.

Lewes watchmaker Thomas Harben made a goodly profit from the wrecked ship. In an issue of *Sussex County Magazine* a Mr R.D. Woodall wrote: 'He [Harben] was a shrewd speculator, and his shrewdest coup was to purchase the salvage rights of the ship. Most of the population between Seaford and Eastbourne were engaged in salvage on their own account: But the valuable quicksilver could not be handled by beachcombers, and Harben recovered almost all of it. Additionally, he was offered salvaged virgin gold ingots at small cost.'

A poem credited to Sussex poet James Hurdis, whose tomb is in Bishopstone church, records the incident:

At length the storm abates

And the returning thunder scarce is heard

Save the grand surge, whose heavy fall sounds awful,

And as it sinks, with hard concession rakes

The flinty beach. A multitude they meet,

Who, one by one, studiously prowl along

The sounding shore, and glean the foamy weed

For hidden wreck.

DARBY'S CAVE – THE FIRST BEACHY HEAD LIGHT

'A scene more strange in Britain don't appear,

At once surprising both the eye and ear:

Westwards from Beachy near four hundred pole,

A cave was cut, is now called Derby's Hole:

As stately piles oft bear their founders' name,

So this same cell perpetuates the fame.

A rev'rend Wight, who left his weekly care,

Chose drudging here for drudgery of prayer;

With axe and pick, he cleft the rugged rock,

He spared no pains, but with flaying stock;

When he had hewn this subterraneous cell,

His lonesome fancy led him there to dwell;

But noxious vapours, which did here collect,

Soon seiz'd the fire, and spoil'd the architect.

Tho' one man loft, twelve Dutchmen by it survives;

Being shipwrecked here, with hardship saved their lives.'

An unknown schoolmaster, c.1787

'Under one of the cliffs is a large cavern, consisting of an opening stair-case, a dining-room and bedchamber, said to be carved or hewn out by a clergyman, taking its name from him, and is called Derby's Hole; from hence, near a mile, is Birling Gap, an ancient gateway shod with iron, being used in former wars, and is a way up to the land. It encloses a hill named Beltout, of a half oval shape.'
From East Bourne and its Environs, attributed to J. Royer, 1799

Jonathan Darby (1667–1726) was rector of East Dean, Friston, Littlington and Wilmington. Born at Appleby-in-Westmorland, he married Ann Segar at the age of 14 in 1681. Two years later they moved to Oxford. He obtained his BA in 1689 and his Master's degree in 1704. He was father to five children: Samuel, Richard, Anne, William and an unnamed baby who died at birth; sadly three more of the children died young. He moved to East Dean in 1692, where he had secured an appointment as curate at Littlington church. Here he busied himself with church affairs, but was aware that poverty was all around him. Smuggling was an accepted way of life to ease the deplorable conditions endured by many. Jonathan was strongly opposed to the locals stripping wrecks, although he was compassionate enough to understand why they did so. If there was a shipwreck, as villagers, carrying baskets, clambered over the rocks looking for salvageable items, Jonathan searched for mariners who might be saved. If he found any bodies he arranged Christian burials.

On 11 February 1705 he was offered the parsonage of Friston and East Dean, and the following year the full-time appointment to East Dean parish, where his family was warmly welcomed. He administered God's comfort to his cherished flock and recorded daily affairs in the parish registers.

After witnessing a number of wrecks and discharging the last rites over many graves of unknown mariners in his churchyard, Jonathan was fired with the urge to give practical help. Working with a pick, chisel and axe, and often wearing his familiar beaverskin hat, he enlarged some caves, rough caverns that had been used by smugglers, under the Belle Tout promontory and about a mile from his home. He hewed out a series of tunnels in the cliff face, reached by a staircase in a chimney-shaped hole from the beach. One visitor, years later, described how they had to clamber up the chimney using notches for their feet, 'whilst holding onto a rope, which was suspended from a ring and staple driven into the chalk above. The chimney would admit just one person. At the top there were four or five roughly cut steps which led to the 'Hall' from where you could look out of an arched window, which Darby had enlarged from its smuggling days. The window was about 50ft above the beach. The Hall would have held up to 35 persons. There were two alcoves in the Hall, one was probably made by smugglers for defence purposes, and the other alcove was used by Darby for his lantern store.'

One of the caves had a balcony some 20ft above highest water, accessed through a chimney from the Downs. Another cave was lit by two lanterns that were set into the wall. It was basically furnished, the walls blackened by candle smoke, and there was a well-worn carpet on the floor. During rough weather Jonathan sat alone in this cold, damp sanctuary, a light fastened above the balcony to warn unsuspecting vessels of the dangers. Ropes and other rescue equipment were stored in side recesses.

Jonathan's bible, kept on a nearby table, was his companion. Opening it, he gave thanks for a safe journey to the cave in treacherous weather, and asked God's blessing 'for those in peril on the sea'. Single-handed, he achieved what many men had only debated – helping to save the lives of many sailors. His was the first Beachy Head 'lighthouse'. The villagers, however, feared that they might lose their lucrative income from stripping wrecks. 'He will have us in the workhouse,' one labourer said in the local Tiger Inn.

After the death on 24 April 1707 of their eldest son Samuel, and the loss of a baby in 1708, Jonathan became increasingly withdrawn and his cave became almost a second home. London journalists mistakenly interpreted this as the result of 'the vinegary tongue of his wife, from which to escape he nightly sought the quiet of his cave existence'.

Jonathan's wife died at the age of 59 in December 1723. Heartbroken and sobbing, he wrote in the church register: 'Mrs Anne Darby. Bury'd Dec 19th wife of Mr Jonathan Darby, Minister.' The tears running down his face dripped onto the paper and mingled with the ink, smudging the first two letters – still visible to this day. With Christmas being celebrated by all those around him, Jonathan could only sit and lament his great loss. He wrote, 'My beloved Anne, my wife, this home is now left to me desolate.'

With no purpose left in life, and the dampness of the cave taking its toll on his health, Jonathan Darby finally collapsed in the late summer of 1726 and was carried to his bed with a raging fever. He lingered until 25 October, when he died in his sleep. He is buried in East Dean churchyard under a re-engraved slab:

Here lies the body of Parson Darby M.A. Oxon

Who died on 26th October 1726

He was the sailors' friend.

Darby's Cave.
(Picture courtesy of East Sussex
Library and Information Services.)

The ravages of the sea eroded the cave and the villagers drifted back into their old ways. Smugglers moved into the remnants of the cavern again, but after a coastguard tower was built nearby they departed to a safer haven at Crowlink Gap. Darby's Cave, or what was left of it, became something of a sightseeing curiosity, with local children earning a penny by leading interested visitors to the spot. With the passing years, however, the memories faded. After cliff falls in 1916 entrance to the cave became almost impossible. The Rev. A.A. Evans, one of Darby's successors, wrote in the 1930s: 'the entrance to the cave is quite washed away, but by means of a ladder the visitor can get within and see the chisel and axe markings clearly visible on the walls.'

One gesture towards saving shipwrecked sailors trapped on the beach by rising tides was the making of an iron cage by a Mr Thunder. This could transport four or five people from the base of the cliff. By using windlasses and pulleys, with capstans fastened in the ground, the two-wheeled trolley was drawn to the cliff edge, securely fixed, and a rope was run over pulleys to let down the basket, so mariners could be hauled up. A 1799 Eastbourne guide, *East Bourne – a descriptive account of the village*, by James Royer, states that the cage was owned by Mr Willard of Birling Farm, but it is not recorded if it ever saved a life. Local rumour, however, suggested it might have helped to move smuggled goods.

In his 1854 book, *The Guide to East bourne and its Environs*, Hopkins states: 'There are other smaller caverns cut in the face of the perpendicular cliff here, more recently by Order of the Corporation of The Trinity House, with a view to afford a chance of escape for shipwrecked persons, who otherwise must inevitably perish, in a storm at high water.'

The Rev. H.E. Maddock MA carried out a survey of the caves of Beachy Head in 1875, and at the entrance to Darby's Hole he discovered a number of inscriptions. One was 'S.R. 1743', another had the date 1788, but the names could not be read.

An army officer named Francis Grose sketched the cave in 1795, indicating that these cave rooms were 'reasonably sized'.

Arthur Beckett wrote in *The Spirit of the Downs* (fifth edition, 1930) that 'Parson Darby's cave is now almost obliterated. I remember, when a boy, climbing into it by means of a rope ladder, which I had made with considerable pride. Darby died in 1726. But his excavation, since it was the means of saving the crew of a Dutch seaman, evidently met with the approval of The Brethren of Trinity House, for, by their orders, a number of other caves were excavated in the neighbourhood, though no record exists of their ability to save lives.'

Jonathan Darby's tomb.
(Picture by Elizabeth Wight)

BELLE TOUT – THE HEADLAND

The name Belle Tout was adopted from the promontory on which the lighthouse was built. Its origins are debatable. Some say that it comes from ancient associations, 'Toot' being Saxon for 'look out' and 'Bel' being a pagan deity. In a 1942 edition of *Sussex County Magazine* a correspondent from Chichester wrote: 'Belle Toute or Beltout? I have not found serious difficulty over Belle Tout. Tout or Toot is a frequent place name for a look-out. Belle is more difficult. Most writers give it a Celtic origin, possibly Baal, for bits of Mediterranean lore reached at least the coastline of this land.' The editor of this magazine mentioned that *The Place Names of Sussex* spells out the name, Belle Tout, but pointed out that in 1724 it was spelt Beltout.

Alfred Watkins in *The Long Straight Track* has it that all names starting with 'Bel' denote places where the god Baal was worshipped. F.W. Bourdillion, writing about Beachy Head, offered his thoughts: 'Tout may be the same word as toat or tote, found in Tote-Hill or Tot-Hill which means a 'look out' or, more probably, it may mean a peak or prominence.'

The Headland. Originally known as Belle Tout Down.
(Picture by Elizabeth Wright.)

The site chosen for the erection of a lighthouse was on a high chalk plateau, which has had an association with mankind for thousands of years. The Downs were formed during the Cretaceous period, roughly 120m–75m years ago. Neolithic man (3000–1850 BC) settled here, as did Bronze Age man after him. The building was once surrounded by three overlapping earthwork enclosures, of which parts of only two remain; they are now designated as a scheduled ancient monument. The larger outer enclosure has historically been regarded as of potentially Iron Age/Romano British in date, and could have been part of a stock corral or a promontory fort. Later tentative reassessments of excavations tended to indicate pastoral use rather than defensive enclosures. Investigations carried out in 1813 by D. Giddy on a barrow in the enclosed area revealed the remains of an Early Bronze Age food vessel containing cremated remains. The barrow, and some of the adjacent land, has since gone into the sea.

The first occupiers of the area were prehistoric hunter-gatherers, who came across from the continent before the formation of the Channel in about 6,500 BC. Their crude dwellings with thatched roofs would have been similar to those discovered on the coasts of France. They may have brought with them domesticated sheep. Excavations around the cliffs have revealed traces of agricultural settlements, bank and ditch enclosures that are over 4,000 years old.

In 1909 H. Toms found the remains of a Beaker People settlement at Belle Tout. These people were so called because of their distinctive pottery that is bell-shaped in profile. They lived in more permanent settlements than their ancestors. The Beaker People seem to have been of a different physical type than earlier populations in the same geographical areas, suggesting that migration from the continent brought them to our shores in about 2500 BC. They integrated into the indigenous population, introducing them to new farming methods, copper working skills, mortuary techniques and other cultural innovations. They influenced Neolithic burial practices, favouring single contracted internments of complete corpses, accompanied by grave goods such as knives, flint arrowheads and pottery beakers. Later excavations suggested that 'Beaker associated activity recorded at Belle Tout – evidence of buildings, a midden, and work areas, within a probable stock enclosure, was associated with a very large domestic Beaker assemblage' (Bradley, 1970, 1982).

Late Neolithic and Early Bronze Age people were drawn to these water-retaining chalk uplands, preferring to work the light, easily cultivated soil rather than the heavy Wealden clays. Downland soils are shallow and drain easily; they warm up quickly after rain. At that time the downland was forested, covered mainly with native beech trees, so these early settlers cleared small areas of woodland using robust flint axes, and, in a primitive form of farming, started to grow crops, such as barley or emmer wheat. Later, as the worked soil became exhausted, livestock, primarily sheep, were grazed on the land and folded in pens at night. Their dung which they spread around and trod in, proved invaluable for keeping the ground well fertilised. Inherited experience taught the downland farmer that this was how to get the best out of the land.

Today's modern, compact Southdown sheep, with the woolly 'teddy bear' look, are far removed from their leaner ancestors, domesticated by Neolithic man. Discovery of sheep bone remains in archaeological digs suggest that these prehistoric short coated, black faced heath sheep had lived on the chalky uplands for centuries. The Southdowns have a naturally laid-back disposition, are hardy, fast maturing and produce meat of an excellent flavour, helped, it is said, by the sheep eating wild thyme and aromatic herbs that grow in the chalky soil.

The boundary of a causewayed enclosure is clearly visible in the circle of shaded turf running up to the cliff edge on the east side of the lighthouse, its continuation and original entrance cut short by falling chalk. Causewayed enclosures, constructed between c.4, 000 and 3300 BC, are the earliest surviving enclosures built in the British Isles, and their function is something of a puzzle. They are not permanent settlements, although pits and groups of holes suggest the presence of some form of structures. *The University of London's Rescue Archaeology in Sussex* (1976) by Peter Drewet, Owen Bedwin and David Freke, lists causewayed enclosures as 'communal/political life and burial', whereas 'open settlements featured domestic/farming life'.

These at Belle Tout contained evidence of domestic complexes and an extensive flint-working industry. There were many Neolithic flints found, including polished axes, leaf-shaped arrowheads, scrapers, cores and flakes. These appear to have been mined, as the quality was far better than flint nodules picked up in the fields, which would have been made brittle from exposure. A small early Bronze Age pot was found in a barrow here.

Arthur Beckett writes about these early tools in *Spirit of The Downs* (1930):
'Stephen Blackmore, an old shepherd, made a valuable collection of Neolithic implements of the neighbourhood ... of Beachy Head, which were found by him on the hills ... while tending sheep during a period extending many years. Blackmore's collection of Neolithic implements is considered to be one of the finest in this country ... I remember several years ago incurring the old man's wrath by reasons of a newspaper article which I wrote concerning this collection, the result of which was, said the owner, that he was 'worried to death by a gen'leman from the Lunnon museum who came down and wanted to buy them, but I wasn't going to sell.'

'Blackmore, although always pleased to show his collection to anyone who expressed the wish, was always jealous of it; and I never knew him inclined to part with any of the best specimens, even when he was badly in need of money, having to live on 10/- a week. His collection contained fine examples of sling stones, arrow-heads of flint, heavy axe heads, a stone pick, a knitting needle, and some specimens of flints worked to a point and probably used for boring purposes.'

Living accommodation for the early settlers consisted of circular huts, each supported by a central pole with smaller posts around the edges. The roofs were thatched with boughs and the walls were made of wattle and daub. The climate was kinder, so such structures were sufficient. All these remains indicate that the headland location appears to have had some local importance at this time.

In *Portrait of Sussex* Cecile Woodford writes: 'On the 16th August, 1909, Mr H.S. Toms, a member of the Eastbourne Natural History Society, commenced excavations at the Belle Tout lighthouse, near Beachy Head. Permission to carry out this project was given by Mr Carew Davies Gilbert, one of Eastbourne's well-known landowners. This was the earliest known excavation of a site which revealed remains of the Bronze Age.'

In a book published by the Sussex Archaeological Society, Lewes, in 1975 there is a brief chapter entitled 'A section through the Iron Age promontory fort at Belle Tout', which records that in a scheme to tidy up Belle Tout the National Trust wished to bury some telegraph wires: 'As the earthworks on Belle Tout are all scheduled under the Ancient Monuments Acts, the Trust gave the Department of the Environment three months' notice of their intention to dig this trench.' A watching brief by Archaeology South-East noted that 'there were no datable finds or evidence of features within the enclosed area'. Further excavations were carried out by the Sussex Archaeological Society in 1968–9: 'It is interesting that the slight earthwork at Belle Tout could only have served as an enclosure to contain livestock and could never be properly defended.'

In *A Mesolithic Assemblage from East Sussex* by Richard Bradbury (Sussex Archaeological Society, Occasional Paper 2) Lawrence Stevens writes: 'The headland is scarred by prehistoric man's activities crowning the promontory like a thin coronet, and once enclosing 50 acres, is a bank and a ditch encircling the old lighthouse.'

Although a small depression near Belle Tout was noted and recorded, no excavations were done until cliff falls in 1971 and 1976 revealed an ancient 144ft deep cylindrical shaft in the chalk cliffs. There were no traces of anything inside, suggesting that 'it may have been hollow for the most part'. It has since been washed away, but speculation abounds that it was a ritual shaft used for sacrifices some 3,000 to 4,000 years ago. There was a series of footholds cut opposite each other in the sides. Tool marks in the face of the chalk appear to have been made with a metal implement with one pointed and one broad end. In antiquity this shaft would have been well inland. In July 1975 further examinations were made, and when gault clay was found a few feet deeper it was then suggested that it might have been a well. Soil samples taken in 1980, with the collector dangling from a helicopter, only contained one shard of Middle Bronze Age pottery.

Retired coastguard Garry Russell, BEM, remarked that during his time protecting this coastline he and his colleagues had found it useful when they were scaling the cliffs.

THE EARLY DAYS

Many sailing ships continued to founder in the area. On 23 January 1789 the *Syren*, a West Indiaman from St Annes, Jamaica, carrying rum, sugar and pimento, was wrecked, although the crew were saved. An advertisement in the *Sussex Weekly Advertiser* stated:

To be sold at Public Sale. On Monday 2nd of March between the hours of 12 to 4 o'clock at the house of Mrs. Kemp, Newhaven, 30 puncheons and some tillages of choice rum (one puncheon in each lot) saved out of the wreck of the ship 'Syren', Thomas Hayman, Master, from Jamaica, stranded near Beechy Head on the 22nd January last (now secured under His Majesty's Officers, at Mr Willard's, East Dean, etc.) subject to Custom House duty of 5d and excise duty of 3/7d per gallon. The purchase money and duties to be paid and the rum taken away within six days after sale – Samples to be seen at Messrs. Dutton and Chapman's, Eastbourne, the casks may be viewed by making application to the proper officers. The samples will be removed to Newhaven three days previous to the date of the Sale.

In the early part of the 19th century a Royal Navy captain, having escaped near-disaster off Beachy Head, vigorously demanded that the Elder Brethren of Trinity House should take action and build a permanent lighthouse, as the seas around Beachy Head presented a serious threat to shipping.

The origins of Trinity House date back to a charitable guild of sea samaritans established by Archbishop Stephen Langton in the 12th century. The first official record is the grant of a royal charter by Henry VIII in 1514 to a fraternity of mariners called the Guild of the Holy Trinity 'So that they might regulate the pilotage of ships in the King's streams'. At the time of its inception this charitable guild owned a great hall and almshouses close to the naval dockyard of Deptford on the River Thames. In 1604 James I conferred on Trinity House rights concerning compulsory pilotage of shipping and the exclusive right to license pilots in the River Thames. The responsibility for district pilotage was transferred to Port and Harbour Authorities under the 1987 Pilotage Act.

Under the Seamarks Act of 1566 Trinity House was given the powers to set up 'So many beacons, marks and signs for the sea whereby the dangers may be avoided and escaped and ships the better come into their ports without peril'. Unfortunately Trinity House funds were extremely limited until in 1594 the Lord High Admiral of England surrendered his rights to the sale of dredged ballast to sailing vessels discharging their cargoes in the port of London. The rights of ballastage passed to Trinity House, who took over responsibility for dredging shingle from the bed of the River Thames and sold it to masters requiring ballastage. With the rapid growth of shipping to the port of London this was a very profitable business, but it declined at the end of the 19th century when steel ships capable of holding seawater ballast were introduced.

The next 200 years saw a proliferation of lighthouses being built, many privately owned, with an annual fee paid either to the Crown or Trinity House. The owners of the private lights were allowed to levy light dues from passing ships when they reached port. The reliability of many of these private lights left much to be desired, and so in 1836 legislation was passed that all private lights in England, Wales and the Channel Islands would be compulsorily purchased and placed under the management of Trinity House. The previous owners were compensated on the basis of their receipts from light dues.

Aids to night navigation in this part of the English Channel were virtually non-existent, and by 1824 the number of ships falling foul of these dangerous waters had risen to epidemic proportions – often helped, it was said, by locals tying lamps around the necks of grazing animals, thus giving the impression that they were vessels moving in safe waters.

On 3 February 1822 a 1,350 ton East Indiaman ship, the *Thames*, sailing from China, hit rocks off Eastbourne and was blown ashore in hurricane force winds. The captain's log stated:

Sunday February 3rd, at ten minutes past 2 a.m. while in the act of steering, weather very thick, ship struck upon a reef a short distance east of Beachy Head, called the Boulder Bank at 3 a.m. There being no chance of getting her off until flood-tide made, nor then to sea, lowered down cutter from the quarter, and attempted to hoist our launch, which attempt (on account of the sea running too high to risk the lives of the men, as well as the cutter having swamped in veering in a storm, by which misfortune six men were drowned), was abandoned. At half past 3 a.m. began to fire signal guns and show lights, and cut away mast to ease ship. At 6 a.m. ship, by violence of the surf, was forced upon the beach near tower 72 in Eastbourne Bay. At 10 a.m. Sea having left ship, opened communication with shore, and ship's company landed with safety; begin to make preparations to land cargo.

The valuable cargo, worth £30,000, was landed on the beach and stacked 'in regular order'. Crowds gathered to watch the drama but nothing was plundered, 'a rare instance in the case of a shipwreck'. Four local fishermen, desperate to help, launched a lugger to try to save the 140 crew members, and six of the ship's crew tried to make their own way ashore in one of the *Thames*'s own boats, but the tiny craft was hit by a huge wave and overturned, resulting in their deaths. A second lugger was put to sea by three more fishermen, together with Midshipman Smith of the Coast Blockade, but this too capsized in the rough seas. Midshipman Smith drowned.

The hull of the *Thames* was severely damaged, but temporarily repaired when 18 shipwrights arrived with caulkers to stop the leaks. Three weeks later tugs *Venus* and *Swift* towed the *Thames* to Gravesend, Kent.

Underwriters conveyed part of the cargo to London at 3s. 4d. per cwt, the rest by water at a cost of 1s. per cwt. It was all sold by auction.

Sketch of the shipwrecked 'The Thames'. (Courtesy of Sussex County Magazine.)

THE SECOND BEACHY HEAD LIGHT

Greatly influenced by continuous shipwrecks and the loss of lives, local MP and squire 'Mad' Jack Fuller (1757–1834), famed as a creator of follies, arranged finance to have a lighthouse built on the 258ft high Belle Tout cliff-top. Fuller, born with a silver spoon in his mouth, was a wealthy country squire, a Member of Parliament and owner of Sussex estates. Well known for his sociable attitude, he enjoyed good food and wine, playing cards and making a few wagers. A friend said, 'He's an upstanding, downsitting sort of man, and when angry, he bellowed like a farmer shouting in a ten acre field.' His weight in later life ballooned to 22 stone, earning him the nickname of Hippo. The closest he came to marriage was when he proposed to Miss Susanna Arabella Thrale, but although he was quite a catch, being rich and well-educated, she turned him down. Once bitten, twice shy, he remained a bachelor for the rest of his life. During his later years he became a much-respected philanthropist.

With Fuller's financial support, a temporary, experimental and much-needed wooden structure came into operation on 1 October 1828, 'with good all round views'.

Parry's 'The Coast of Sussex,' published in 1833 stated; 'Further on, to the right, is the lighthouse on a projecting neck of land, capable of being seen at a much greater distance by mariners when coming within distance of the shore. It has been erected of late years, though seemingly called for long before.'

This temporary building appeared to be successful, as the number of shipwrecks decreased, so Trinity House decided to replace it with a permanent building. In recent years they have said that 'there is very little information available on the early wooden structure.' The author of *History and Antiquities of the County of Sussex* wrote: 'The present lighthouse is a temporary building erected by way of an experiment, but as it is found to answer the best hopes of its projectors, a more substantial stone fabric is now in progress.'

BELLE TOUT - THE THIRD BEACHY HEAD LIGHT

Behind the scenes Trinity House had been working on plans for a proper replacement lighthouse. Its Committee of Elders instructed consultant engineers James Walker and John Burges to prepare the necessary documents of design, specifications and estimates.

James Walker (1781–1862) only became a civil engineer by accident. In the summer of 1800 he went to stay with his uncle Ralph Walker, an engineer who was involved with work on the West India docks. James was engrossed with all this and, anxious to learn more, was articled to his uncle in 1803. When Ralph Walker died, James became an engineer to the East India Dock Company, and went on to be an elected member of the Institute of Civil Engineers in 1823. In 1830 he took Alfred Burgess into partnership, and by 1853 the company was Walker, Burges and Cooper. James first worked for Trinity House in 1824 and continued to be associated with them until just before his death. Initially appointed as inspector-general of lights, he was later promoted to consulting engineer, designing and building most of the important lighthouses, including Belle Tout.

In May 1826 Trinity House presented all the required documents to the Lords of the Privy Council, which included the formal application for a Letters Patent, thus allowing a compulsory levy (a toll) to be imposed on passing shipping to pay for the upkeep of the proposed lighthouse. By October the application and required funds were approved. In the meantime Sussex architect William Hallett had converted the scribbled designs provided by James Walker into working drawings. The building, it was stated, 'was to be constructed from Scottish granite, with the keeper's small, single storey cottage built from locally quarried limestone masonry'.

To be effective, warning lights must be high enough to be seen by shipping before danger is reached. The minimum height is calculated by taking the square root of the height of the lighthouse in feet and multiplying it by 1.17 to yield the distance to the horizon in nautical miles. In this case, however, no one had taken into consideration the collapsing coastline.

Building started on Belle Tout lighthouse in 1829, using Aberdeen granite blocks for the walls. This stone was hard-wearing, strong and largely unaffected by erosion, pollution or atmospheric attack.

For some years Aberdeen had enjoyed extensive coastal shipping services with many east coast ports, London in particular, because of the increasing market for granite. Granite made excellent ballast and was transported at favourable rates, generally 8s. per ton (in 1835) by vessels belonging to the Aberdeen Navigation Company, the London Shipping Company and the Aberdeen and Hull Shipping Company. After offloading in London, vessels then went to Sunderland 'and at that port receive cargoes of coal for Aberdeen. By this means the coals are sold in Aberdeen at about 5 per cent cheaper than if no granite was transported by the same shipping; and consequently the stone is afforded cheaper than if no coals were conveyed to Aberdeen.'

Graeme Robertson, MD of A and J Robertson (Granite) Ltd tentatively suggested that Rubislaw quarry in Aberdeen might have been the supplier of granite for Belle Tout, 'because it was the largest and most productive quarry in the area [at that time]. It is likely that the granite blocks were dressed in the quarry to make them more easily handled during shipping. The blocks probably went to the port of Maidstone because that was where the ship was destined; these blocks were used as ballast which allowed transport at preferential rates.'

When the barges docked at Maidstone the granite was transferred onto wagons, which were then hauled by oxen across the county to Beachy Head. Oxen were hardy, ideal draught animals that could thrive under the most adverse conditions. In normal working circumstances teams of either four, six or eight, when hitched to a wagon, could accomplish in a slow and plodding manner as much work as a team of horses, but more economically. Their cloven hooves were ideal for coping with the heavy Wealden clays, their tread pulverising the soil.

BEACHY HEAD LIGHT HOUSE, NEAR EAST BOURN.
Published by M. Heatherly.

Sketch by M. Heatherly – 'The Beachy Head Light House, near East bourn
(Courtesy of Sussex County Magazine.)

The Weald was still well wooded, and the few available roads, little more than tracks in some areas, were in a deplorable condition. In winter they were covered in thick mud, known locally as stodge or slab, with deep water-filled holes that only the oxen had the strength to pull carts through, and in summer the tracks were hard, rutted and axle-breaking.

A rather far fetched local tale indicates that the roads were in an appalling state. It tells of a traveller who found a hat lying in the mud. On picking it up he found a man underneath. Asked if he needed help to get out, the buried man replied, 'Never mind me, start looking for my horse and cart!'

Julian Bell, curator of the Weald and Downland Open Air Museum, has made some suggestions about the type of wagon that might have been used to transport the granite blocks, although he acknowledges that there are no definitive answers:

'There were in existence specific wagons used for moving stone, but they in turn were probably adapted from timber carriages which would have been more common in the south east of England. Such carriages were low slung vehicles of a very strong but simple structure comprising two axles linked by a pole; extra poles or boards would be laid between the axles in order to facilitate the transport of stone blocks.

What would have been more likely is that for such a one-off job local vehicles of any appropriate nature would have been employed. These would probably have been standard farm box wagons which were the general purpose workhorse of rural areas, and whose characteristics altered from one geographic area to another – so there were Kent wagons and Sussex wagons available in that area. These two types of wagon were fairly similar in appearance and construction and generally came equipped with single width hooped wheels; for extra heavy loads or where the ground was less supportive, double width wheels were used.'

In an article on farm wagons J. Hutchins writes in the 1929 issue of the *Sussex County Magazine*: 'The wagons represent the outcome of long ages of experiment, experience and hereditary skill. During this process all superfluous material has been eliminated to reduce weight to the lowest limit consonant with strength and rigidity; the actual forms and dimensions of the various members have been arrived at by a long process of trial and error, during which unsuitable shapes and methods of construction have been discarded. On dry chalk soil the width of the wheels is comparatively narrow; while on the retentive clays the tyres are frequently double the width.'

David Viner, author of *Wagons and Carts* (2008) and *Roads, Tracks and Turnpikes* (2007), suggests that 'large blocks of stone make for heavy loads, so my guess is that this would be done via workmanlike two-wheeled carts rather than the heavier, four wheeled wagons. The wagon is much more usually associated with agricultural processes and less as road vehicles. Carts, on the other hand, are the workhorses for such loads.'

Dr. Oliver Douglas, assistant curator at the Museum of English Rural Life, wrote: 'We have a Sussex wagon on display, but it stems from a farming context ... I think it is a fairly narrow gauge and unlikely to have been robust enough to cope with the kind of heavy work described. My guess is that something heavier, possibly with straked wheels, might have been more appropriate.'

Daniel Defoe, when writing about the unpleasant Wealden mud that formed an almost impassable barrier: 'I have seen one tree on a carriage which they call a tug, drawn by twenty-two oxen, and even then it is taken but a small way.'

Belle Tout at night.
(Picture courtesy of East Sussex Library and Information Services.)

When finally finished, the lighthouse was 47ft high and some 20ft in diameter. Martin Boyle writes in *Beachy Head: Lighthouses of England and Wales* that, 'Compared to other lighthouses constructed around the same period, Belle Tout consisted of a squat circular structure, with the keeper's quarters erected at the rear. The tower ... had a cast iron lantern. Its conical roof was formed out of cast iron rafters covered with sheets of copper. In turn, this was topped by a tall copper chimney, along with a wind vane and a lightning conductor spike.'

Belle Tout was just about completed in 1831, but it took until 11 October 1834 before the lamp was first lit. Belle Tout's reflectors and Argand fountain lamps were combined on a platform which revolved every two minutes, throwing a light of 22,000 candle power that could be seen 23 miles out to sea. The light used 2 gallons of oil an hour. A guidebook issued in 1878 invited visitors to 'inspect the massive Belle Tout lighthouse with its thirty oil lamps'.

The *Illustrated London News* of 5 January 1884, under the heading 'Inside Belle Tout', carried the following article:

At the eastern extremity of the South Downs, on the Sussex coast, the grand promontory of Beachy Head, near Eastbourne, rises to a height of 575 feet above the sea. On the Belle Tout cliff, which projects forward at a much less elevation, stands the lighthouse, erected between 1828 and 1831 ... The tower is 47ft high, and the lantern displays a revolving light, every two minutes, visible at the distance of 23 miles. The apparatus here employed is that of the 'catoptrics' system, in which a revolving frame has a number of large concave reflectors, with an Argand fountain lamp in each, fitted to each side of the frame. The shape and position of the reflectors are precisely calculated, to throw the rays of light, in a combined flood of light, upon certain parts of the surface of the sea, and to prevent their being wasted in the sky. The reflectors are formed with a parabolic curve, internally, and are constructed of sheet copper, with a plating of silver on the inner side, which is kept bright and clean by the use of polishing powder (rouge, or trioxide of iron) and by frequent rubbing with a piece of soft chamois leather. One of the keepers ... applied the powder with a fine brush of camel's hair. Great care is always taken to prevent dust or grease remaining in the interior of the lighthouse, as it would be apt to spoil the reflectors. The Argand lamps have cotton circular wicks of an inch diameter, or sometimes double circular concentric wicks; and are fed with Colza oil [rape seed oil] from a metal canister behind each reflector. This is the ordinary apparatus of a white revolving light; but there is a special arrangement for flashing lights, and for intermittent lights, in which the illumination bursts forth suddenly, and continues steadily for a certain time, after which it is suddenly eclipsed. The ordinary revolving light gradually increases to its maximum, and then diminishes gradually to total darkness. When a powerful fixed light is required, it is produced by an apparatus on the dioptric system with Plano convex lenses, formed in concentric circles, filling a large sheet of glass, by which the rays of light are refracted and directed towards the sea. This was the invention of the French engineer, J.A. Fresnel, about 60 years ago; but several improvements and adaptations have since been introduced, and the 'holophotal' system of Mr T. Stevenson has brought it almost to perfection.

The Argand hollow wick lamp and parabolic reflector was introduced in about 1810 by Winslow Lewis, and whale oil may have been used before Colza oil.

The revolving pedestal rotated by means of a clockwork mechanism powered by a hanging heavy weight, which required rewinding to the top of the tower every two hours. This was a back-breaking feat for the keepers, who also had to trim wicks, replenish fuel, clean the lenses and perform other maintenance tasks.

Very little air circulated inside the lantern, owing to a design fault. Each of the lamps had small exhaust pipes that led into the chimney flue, but the air became stale, affecting the keeper's breathing, and condensation built up on the internal face of the lantern. This led to a distortion of the light's rays, and passing ships had to cope with reduced night-time visibility. Another problem was that the cowl on the top of the chimney was fixed and facing landward, which meant that a change of wind direction caused the exhaust fumes to blow back into the lantern. Michael Faraday, scientific officer for Trinity House, put together a system of vents, with a geared mechanism operated by a wind vane that rotated the cowl, to overcome the problem.

Lewes stonemason company Parsons, which later became C.F. Bridgman, supplied the following to Belle Tout lighthouse on 11 June 1842:

40 tons of Pitches @ 8/6d per ton (£17/-/-d) plus carriage of £18/15/-

Paid carter for carriage @ £7/-/-d

Paid Preventative Men £2/14/-d

Townsend 8 days wages @ £2/4/8d

Wright 8 days wages @ £1/8/-d

Labourers £1/7/3d

Total Bill being £58/-/-1d.

Belle Tout with lighthouse keeper and family.
(Picture courtesy of East Sussex Library and Information Services.)

Lighthouse keepers in residence during Belle Tout's active life were the following:

1835–6: S.L. Howard.
1841: T. Griffiths. S. Comber.
1851: W. Colerein.
1851–2: J. Pierce.
1861: T. Hattam. G. Faulkner.
1863–8: G. Staples.
1865–6: T. Hattam.
1868–71: G.W. Brown.
1871–6: W. Grimmer.
1875–9: C.A. Barnby.
1876–9: R. Wooden.
1879–87: J.G. Grainger.
1881: C.A. Barnby.
1887–90: A. Belt (senior)
1888–91: J. Fisher.
1891: T.H. Blowey.
1902: G.G. Smith and J.W. Parsons.

1874

1909

1890

1920

1902

LATE
1920's

Composition of old pictures of Belle Tout. (Pictures courtesy of
Sussex County Magazine and East Sussex Library and Information Services.)

In 2010 K. Southall, searching for ancestors on the internet, commented: 'Family members in Devon or Cornwall either joined the Navy, were fishermen or merchants. One became assistant lighthouse keeper at Belle Tout ... But I found an anomaly in the 1891 census, whereby both he and his family, and the lighthouse keeper and family were listed twice. Once at the lighthouse, once at East Dean. It looks like the enumerator was aware of this as there is a comment on one of the listings.'

In *Untold Stories – Beachy Head*, Sheila Ryan writes about the memories of Barbara Scott, whose great grandfather, Chessman Barnby, was made chief lighthouse keeper on 20 January 1874. His daughter Emily Barnby, one of 10 children, kept a diary. She noted that they kept chickens and a pig, and bought milk from a local farm. Her father grew vegetables in the garden so the family was mostly self- sufficient: 'the pig was killed in the garden and hung up in the shed before being treated ... It was a nasty smelly business. There was fat to tender down, for lard, yards of sausages to prepare and make, spare ribs to bake, the stomach to clean and fill with pudding mixture and boil.' She mentioned that the wreck of a vessel broke up nearby with a mixed cargo of oranges, barrel bungs, corks and nutmegs, all of which were scattered along the shore. There was enough wood from the ship to make good their garden fences. Their father couldn't afford 6d a week for each of the smaller children to go to school, so they spent their days happily playing on the cliff top. But by April 1888, 58-year-old Chessman became so ill after having a stroke that he retired, and the family moved from Belle Tout to Ramsgate.

Soon after it became operational, it became obvious that Belle Tout had been defectively sited. Although on a clear day its light could be seen some 25 miles away, when the many sea mists (known locally as frets) swirled around the cliffs the light was compromised, and was considered to be 'useless as a navigational aid'. In 1843 Captain William Cole, Lloyd's agent at Newhaven, gave evidence before a Select Committee on Shipwrecks, said that in his opinion Birling Gap remained one of the worst spots on the coast. Mariners groping their way along the Sussex coastline used Belle Tout as a navigational reference: if they could see its flashing light they were a safe distance from the dangerous reefs at the foot of Beachy Head. If the light suddenly disappeared a swift change of course was indicated. But, as previously mentioned, this depended upon the light being set at a carefully calculated distance from the cliff edge. Unfortunately, over 60 years the continuing cliff erosion reduced the original 100ft. The lighthouse had been sited near a major geological fault, so the seas had undermined the cliffs and weakened sections continued to fall onto the beach.

In spite of this, in 1846 Trinity House gave Belle Tout a makeover, with ventilators being added into the lantern and a second storey being built onto the keeper's cottage. Although Belle Tout was much closer to the cliff edge, in 1859 a Dr Gladstone, accompanied by fellow Commissioners for Buoys, Beacons and Lights, checked the site and disarmingly reported, 'It is a first class establishment in excellent order.' They appeared more interested in the principal keeper's complaint that small stones 'were frequently being blown against the lantern in high winds with such velocity that they left tiny holes in the thick plate glass panels'.

Belle Tout c.1900.
(Picture courtesy of Sue Houlihan)

Ships continued to founder. On 19 October 1853 the 800 ton *Dalhousie*, a British full-rigged sailing vessel travelling from London to Sydney with 46 crew and 13 passengers, came into view of Belle Tout. When the freshening south-easterly wind increased to gale force the vessel, chartered by the 'White Horse Line of Australian passenger ships', began to labour. The crew started to throw the deck cargo overboard, but as they did a huge wave washed over the vessel, taking with it a longboat full of livestock. At 5.30am the *Dalhousie* rolled right over onto her starboard side and began to sink. According to the sole surviving crew member, cook and carpenter, 22-year-old Joseph Reed, 'The *Dalhousie* had shown herself to be a lively, manageable, ship, behaving remarkably well; consequently it is difficult to account for her behaviour after 4pm.'

The ship's master, John Butterworth, then saw a schooner, the *William*, heading towards them. He told the few survivors to do what they could to save themselves. By the time the *William* was close there were few crew and passengers still alive. The *William*'s crew instructed the survivors to swim towards their vessel, which was totally impossible as the schooner was drifting faster than a man could swim. After two hours and no rescues the *William* sailed away. Other vessels also failed to help, and one by one the survivors died. Joseph Reed was finally rescued by the brig *Mitchel Grove* and put ashore at Dover. The foundering of the *Dalhousie* was attributed to bad stowage of cargo, which made her top-heavy.

The stranding in 1876 of the British steamship *Rubens* en route from Buenos Aires to Antwerp, with a cargo of wool and hides valued at £150,000, was a further example of the ineffectiveness of Belle Tout's light. The vessel, with forty-two crew aboard, ran aground in thick fog under the lighthouse, still sounding her whistle to warn others of her presence. In spite of throwing 200 bales of wool overboard to make the vessel lighter, and the efforts of two steam tugs from Newhaven to pull her free, she remained grounded. The Newhaven lifeboat, *Elizabeth Boys*, stood by for the next two days and night in case help was needed, as there was a small hole in the hull that let in some 4in of water.

A representative of Her Majesty's Customs at Newhaven, Mr Dolan, came to assess the situation of the valuable cargo. Its removal in the space of 60 hours was suggested, using tugs, barges, muscle power and determination. Only part of it had been removed before the ship's owners, Lamport and Holt from Liverpool, called a halt to the proceedings. A Lewes business, Elphick and Son, was sent a telegram asking for assistance with the removal of the rest of the cargo, at a price of £2 a bale, to be landed at Newhaven. But when they arrived with men and barges they were told that the owners had dropped the price to 5s a bale – so they all returned to Lewes. Other barge owners refused to become involved as *Rubens*'s owners wouldn't pay for insurance cover. However, a band of men from Newhaven eventually moved the cargo for an acceptable agreed sum. The bales thrown overboard were collected by local fishermen, who claimed the salvage money.

The *Eastbourne Gazette* reported on 2 February 1876 that, 'During the afternoon of Thursday, two powerful steam tugs arrived from Dover, and at high water succeeded in getting the vessel off her 'rocky bed' and towing her safely into dock at Southampton, where we are informed she will undergo the necessary repairs. It is reported a court of enquiry into the conduct of the captain, will be held at Southampton on Thursday.'

On 21 February 1876 the 633 ton barque *Coonatto*, en route from Adelaide to London and carrying a cargo of wool, kangaroo skin, bark and some 7,000 copper ingots, went ashore at Crowlink in thick fog. The crew were instructed to leave the vessel at low tide, as the ship was under the control of agents. The following day the tugs *Victoria* and *Orleans* got a line on the *Coonatto*, but after a few attempts to refloat her, the cables snapped. It was decided to lighten the vessel by offloading the cargo and anything else that was salvageable, and then try to get it off the rocks again. But a gale blew up, turning the vessel broadside to the sea. At each high tide it was pushed further inshore. The Receiver of Wrecks described her position as 'very dangerous ... strong wind dead on land,' and with the now swollen waterlogged wool still on board the decking started to burst open, letting some

Belle Tout's lantern. 1884.
(Picture courtesy East Sussex Library and Information Services.)

12in of water into her hull. Subsequent rough tides bumped the vessel around, causing further damage. As no lighter could get alongside, Lloyd's Newhaven agent, Captain Knight, prepared to land the cargo on the cliff. This was a dangerous operation as parts of the hull planking had sprung, so water was flowing freely through the vessel: he noted, 'Sails been unbent and landed and topsail yards sent down. Bower anchor [spare anchor] laid out well upon the bar seaward to keep vessel from drifting further up.' On 24 February at 3pm Knight reported: 'Commence discharging immediately' and at 6.10pm '566 ingots landed. No barge could beach today ... a derrick [steam-driven] on cliff ready. No hope for ship.' The following day he wrote: '600 ingots of copper and a few bags of bark have been landed. Commence discharging wool this morning.' The cargo was put into the charge of the Coastguard. On 26 February: 'Up to last night ex. Coonatto – 149 bales of wool, 20 bags bark, 566 copper ingots ... 6th March ... 5.34pm...Large quantity of loose wool salved. Diver only got 7 cakes copper today, owing to mass [of] iron beams etc and bags copper dross over the cargo. 8th March ...'2,368 bales wool, 374 cakes and 2,041 ingots copper saved ... 30 bales (approx) of loose wool.'

After a week of removing the goods it was found that the *Coonatto* was breaking up, and copper ingots and wool were washed up along the coast. The ship ended up a wreck, and an auction was held on the beach by J.C. Towner to dispose of its various fittings.

Coonatto's master, John Eilbeck Hillman (the third of her three captains, after Smart and 'Beastie' Wilson Begg, so-called because of his cruel treatment of some of the crew), was found to be responsible for poor navigation, and he had his master's certificate suspended for three months. At the Lloyd's enquiry it was stated that, 'the Light of Beachy Head [Belle Tout] was not to have been seen. The discovery of bright shore lights ... appears to have been the first indication of danger, but even this warning does not appear to have awakened the Captain to a sense of his position; five valuable minutes were allowed to elapse before the vessel's course was altered.' It pointed out that no depth readings were taken, 'which appeared to the court inexplicable, seeing that the vessel had run her distance, and the fine light of Beachy Head was still invisible'.

Local rumours abounded that the Coonatto may have been deliberately wrecked for the insurance money, but it was never proved. Known in the marine fraternity as a 'wet ship', she was over-laden and over-canvassed. She has some historical significance because she was made in the London shipyard of John Bilbe in 1863, when the hull construction of large ships was moving from wood to iron and engine power was replacing wind and sail power. She was both iron-framed and timber-framed but still powered by sail, and very much designed for speed. Her fine figurehead was recovered and later placed in the gardens of Birling Manor, being sold to an American in 1970. Her remains, bits of iron and teak, now lie scattered among the rocks below the Seven Sisters cliffs.

One of the most dramatic shipwrecks took place on 25 November 1883 when the New Brunswick of Brevic, a Norwegian three-masted sailing barque carrying cargo from Quebec to West Hartlepool, was driven towards Beachy Head cliffs in hurricane-force winds. By dropping two anchors the vessel was successfully halted for a while. But the force of the winds, coupled with ripped sails, caused the anchors to drag, and the New Brunswick began heading towards dangerous rocks. As sightseers gathered on the cliff top and beach the Newhaven lifeboat crew was mustered, and attempted to leave the harbour. Unfortunately the strength of the winds and the high seas made this impossible. The steam tug Tipper, which usually towed the lifeboat out to sea, wasn't prepared, and it would have taken too long for it to get up a head of steam.

Mr H. M. Emery, the RNLI's honorary secretary in Eastbourne, reported; 'at around 10.45 am intelligence reached here [Eastbourne] that a large foreign barque was riding to her anchor off Belle Tout lighthouse with a signal of distress flying and in a very dangerous position.' So, it was decided that the Eastbourne lifeboat, William and Mary, should be launched. But not from the town's beach, but from Birling Gap, a decision made to avoid heading straight into gale force winds, and struggling through four miles of mountainous seas. But this involved an arduous journey over the downs. The

Belle Tout c.1890's.
(Picture courtesy of East Sussex Library and Information Services.)

crew and some two hundred volunteers hoisted the lifeboat onto its carriage and hauled it to South Street. Here six horses were hitched up. At Meads, 'three additional horses were procured from Mr M. Mockett, of Meadshouse, and with this extra power speedily mounted the hill and crossed the Downs to Birling Gap, a distance of five miles.' The path they were following began to narrow, so a gang of men started digging out the sides, whilst others took the lifeboat off its carriage, and aided by planks of wood used as slides, they got to Birling Gap. Here they found the last few yards of path leading to the beach had been washed away. A make-shift ramp was made from 'some long pieces of timber which were fortunately on the spot ... Under the special superintendence of the Coxswain, and by great exertions, she was got safely down to the beach, and was launched from the shore at 1.15. In charge were Coxswain C. Hide [Charles 'Bones' Hide], second Coxswain Matthews with a crew of fourteen hands.' They rowed through mountainous seas towards the New Brunswick, which took 45 minutes, baling out the water that was filling up the boat.

Having got to the stricken vessel, but unable to come alongside, the best that could be done, was to attach a line to her, and Captain Tobeassin and 14 crew dropped into the sea, to be hauled out by the lifeboat. With everyone safely ashore, the lifeboat had to return the way it had come. The next day the Tipper was able to refloat the New Brunswick and tow her into harbour. 'The rescued crew who appeared in a very exhausted state, one also having sustained a fracture of the ribs, were taken to the C.G. Station and received every attention from the Chief Officer and men, the lifeboat was got up the Gap with considerable difficulty, and reached home about 7.30.'

Even though it was obvious that Belle Tout was of only limited help to shipping, Beachy Head and the lighthouse proved to be a great visitor attraction.

Hopkins, in his 1854 *Guide to Eastbourne and its Environs*, wrote:

For an excursion to the top of Beachy Head, a fine day should be chosen; for when the clouds hang low they rest upon these lofty hills and veil the whole prospect; the effect of this phenomenon is striking, but, of course, the beauty is lost ... the appearance of the light in the Bell Tout Light House warns us that it is time to think of returning. Ladies, and those to whom a pedestrian excursion to Beachy Head would be too fatiguing, may hire a carriage at the Sea Houses ... saddle horses and donkeys too; and donkey chaises are in much request for this favourite jaunt.

Let us proceed to the hill known as Bell Tout, noticing the Light-House erected thereon; the usefulness of which, to those navigating the Channel, has been before alluded to. It is a very massive building – from sunset to sunrise a revolving light is exhibited from the lantern, the revolution occupying six minutes. The maximum brilliancy of the illumination is very great, but diminishes gradually until the light wholly disappears for about three quarters of a minute, and this it continues increasing and diminishing alternatively throughout the night. The light is produced by 30 lamps.

Ward Lock and Co, in their 1913 issue of 'Illustrated Guide to Eastbourne, Pevensey and Seaford' suggest that Beachy Head could also be accessed by char-a-banc at 10.30am (one shilling per person,) at 2.30pm (one shilling and sixpence.) Alternatively by hackney carriage from any public stand to the summit, with half an hour there, the charge for four persons was six shillings.

Further cliff erosion soon started to threaten the lighthouse, as the *Eastbourne Gazette* of 6 January 1875 noted: 'There is a rumour that Belle Tout Lighthouse is in danger in consequence of the encroachment of the sea, and that it is to be pulled down. Whether the present structure is to be pulled down or replaced by a new lighthouse erected on the shore at low water mark, remains to be seen.' There was a heavy fall of chalk, 85,000 tons, from the cliff in 1893, three years later an even larger loss and by 1896 the distance between the lighthouse and the cliff edge was just 70ft.

There had been constant and regular complaints to Trinity House about the times when fog rendered Belle Tout's light virtually useless as a navigation aid, especially between May and October. Experiments

FIGUREHEAD FROM 'COONATTO' IN A GARDEN AT EASTDEAN – REFURBISHED FOR CORONATION OF PRESENT QUEEN. FIGUREHEAD NOW IN AMERICA.

Figurehead from 'Coonatto'.
(By kind permission of Newhaven Maritime Museum.)

proved that a light placed close to the surface of the water was far more successful, so in July 1899 work began at the foot of the cliffs on the erection of the present Beachy Head lighthouse. British Listed Buildings states that Trinity House abandoned Belle Tout in 1899, and until the new lighthouse was finished in 1902 positioned a light vessel off Beachy Head with its own fog horn apparatus.

On 16 April 1902 an article in the *Eastbourne Gazette* stated: 'A newly issued notice to mariners from Trinity House says that it is intended that on or about 2nd October next, to exhibit from sunset to sunrise a white flashing light from the new Beachy Head lighthouse and to establish an explosive fog signal there. The light from the present lighthouse at Belle Tout will be discontinued.'

The light from Belle Tout finally went out on 27 September 1902. Despite its redundancy, it was decided not to demolish the building. On Thursday 2 October 1902 Belle Tout was formally decommissioned, and put up for sale as 'a small, substantial 3-storey building.'

Pencil drawing by Mr. Alexander Robertson, local Secretary of the Eastbourne Branch of the RNLI. 'Launch of the Eastbourne lifeboat at Birling Gap – Nov. 28th 1883 to go to the aid of the Norwegian Barque 'New Brunswick.'. (Picture courtesy of Sussex County Magazine)

BELLE TOUT – A RESIDENTIAL BUILDING

The Corporation of Trinity House sold Belle Tout for £200 to local landowner, Carew Davies Gilbert on 15 June 1903. The hand written Document of Conveyance states:

the Corporation pursuant to the powers and authorities hereto enabling them and as beneficial owners hereby convey unto the said Carew Davies Gilbert all that piece of land situated on Belle Tout Down, near Beachy Head, in the parish of Eastdean and County of Sussex with the lighthouse and buildings and fixtures erected thereon which premises are more particularly delineated on the plan ... IN WITNESS – whereof the said Master Wardens and Assistants [of the Corporation of Trinity House] have caused their Common Seal to be hereunto affixed and the said Carew Davies Gilbert hath hereunto set his hand and seal the day and year first above written.

When Carew Davies Gilbert died in 1913, his married daughter, Patricia Davies Harding, inherited the lighthouse. She was the wife of Charles Henry Harding of Penhale, Truro, Cornwall, a major in the Army. On 8 June 1917 she sold it to Sir Howard George Frank, of 20 Hanover Square, London, for £430. This price included the right of way of an access road for 'horses, carts and motors'. The agreement for the sale stated that 'payment of the purchase money shall take place on the twenty sixth day of June next at the office of Norfolk House, Thames Embankment, London, of Messrs. Williams & James, the Vendor's Solicitors ... Upon completion of the purchase, the purchaser shall be entitled to vacant possession ... and shall be liable for all outgoings as from that date ... The property hereby agreed to be sold forms part of property devised to the Vendor by the Will of her father Carew Davies Gilbert, deceased.'

In a Declaration dated 28 June 1917 Patience Davies Harding wrote:

The freehold in possession free from encumbrances of the said piece of land with the said lighthouse thereon was conveyed to my father the late Carew Davies Gilbert by the Corporation of Trinity House in consideration of a sum of two hundred pounds on the fifteenth day of June One

Front page of Conveyance document of Belle Tout from Trinity House to Carew Davies Gilbert.
(Picture courtesy of David Shaw)

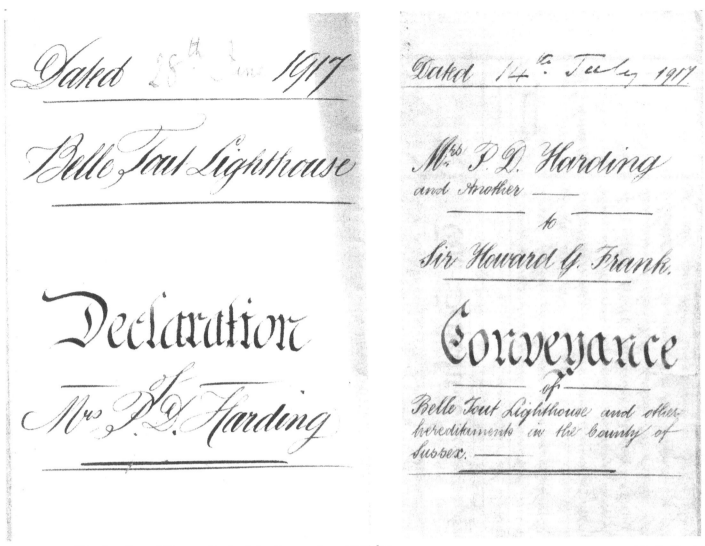

Front page of Declaration of Ownership by Inheritance document for sale of Belle Tout from Mrs. P. Harding to Sir Howard G. Frank.
(Picture courtesy of David Shaw)

Front page of Conveyance document of Belle Tout to Sir Howard G. Frank from Mrs. P.D. Harding.
(Picture courtesy of David Shaw)

thousand nine hundred and three and by his Will dated the ninth day of October One thousand nine hundred and thirteen was devised by my said Father to me.

I well remember my said Father acquiring the said piece of land and lighthouse (I being at the time upwards of twenty years of age) and since the said fifteenth day of June One thousand nine hundred and three, my Father till his death and since his death, his legal personal representatives and latterly myself, have had uninterrupted possession of the said property and no adverse claim of any nature or kind has ever been made against or admitted by my said Father or his said representatives or by myself in respect ... of my title as respective freeholders free from encumbrances.

Sir Howard George Frank (1871–1932) was born at Blackhurst, near Tunbridge Wells, Kent, and educated at Marlborough College. He entered the estate agency business, eventually becoming head of the firms of Knight, Frank and Rutley of London, and Walton and Lee of Edinburgh, as well as president of the Estate Agents Institute from 1912 to 1914 – the year in which he was knighted. In 1916 Sir Howard was appointed honorary adviser to the Ministry of Munitions for land valuation. Shortly afterwards he was appointed Director-General of Lands to the War Office and Air Ministry. Frank was created Baronet of Withyham in the 1920 Birthday Honours for his services in wartime and appointed Knight Grand Cross of the Order of the British Empire in 1924. There appears to be no record of the time he spent at Belle Tout.

SIR JAMES AND LADY PURVES-STEWART

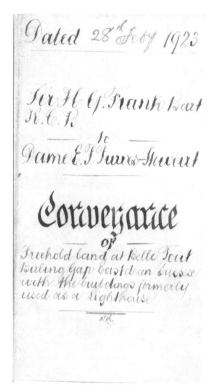

Front page of document of Conveyance of Belle Tout from Sir H. G. Frank to Dame E. P. Purves-Stewart. (Picture courtesy of David Shaw)

Sir James and Lady Purves-Stewart at Belle Tout in 1938. (Picture courtesy of Sue Houlihan)

On 28th February 1923 Belle Tout was purchased for £1,500 by Dame Elizabeth Phipps Purves-Stewart, the wife of distinguished neurologist Sir James Purves-Stewart, KCMG, CB, MD (1869–1949). Sir James, the son of a master tailor in Edinburgh, wrote a number of books, including *Diagnosis of Nervous Diseases* in 1906, but was probably better known for his controversial articles on voluntary euthanasia, which he wrote in the 1930s.

Looking for a weekend retreat, they saw an advertisement for the sale of Belle Tout, motored down from London, liked it and purchased what Sir James described as, 'A solid, square, little granite building with a glass-domed circular lantern tower of copper, fifty feet high, partially surrounded by a dwelling house.' They went about constructing a good wide access road; installed an electric generator in one of the chalk caves and added another storey to the building, as well as, according to later resident Sue Houlihan (née Cullinan), wings for bathrooms. Water came from surface water tanks beneath the courtyard, later being obtained from an artesian well that was sunk 260ft through the cliff.

Before the Purves-Stewarts purchased the building, they had been assured by geologists that Belle Tout would not be affected by cliff erosion for a great number of years. In *Sands of Time: The Recollections of a Physician in Peace and War* (1939) Sir James wrote: '*Soon after taking possession we read a warning article in the local press stating that owing to coastal erosion, grave fears were entertained for the safety of the lighthouse. We decided to secure expert advice. A professor of geology came down from London and, after examining the position, informed us that coastal erosion was undoubtedly going on at a steady rate, and that at the end of six hundred years our tower would find itself at the very edge of the cliff.*' This deduction appears to have been partly based on measurements showing Belle Tout to be 111ft from the cliff edge in 1835 and 98ft in 1890.

A literary critic reviewing *Sands of Time* in a 1940 edition of the *Sussex County Magazine* wrote:

I have been reading a book recently published by a distinguished medical specialist, Sir James Purves-Stewart, who, with lady Purves-Stewart, has for twenty or more years lived at the Old Lighthouse, which edges the Belle Tout headland, the most prominent home in Sussex. I would call it, a sea mark and a land mark. There they dwell as far as the claims of London medical schools and many patients allow.

The book is the story of a life varied, crowded with colour, and lived to the full ... It follows his afterwork through years of energetic effort and ventures in the great London hospitals, nerve clinics, Harley Street and patients, a few rich, many more poor. There are the battlefields;

for Sir James was called by the Government to assist in all the great campaigns – South Africa, the Four Year's War, when he was stationed at Malta, Gallipoli, Egypt and Salonika ... There are visits to Soviet Russia and Nazi Germany. Sir James met all sorts, men of importance at the top, and no less interesting, ordinary, humble folk at the bottom.

In March 1935, the year of his Silver Jubilee, King George V and Queen Mary visited the lighthouse while His Majesty was convalescing in complete privacy at Compton Place in nearby Eastbourne, lent to them by the Duke and Duchess of Devonshire. The town had been recommended by his Majesty's medical advisers 'as a most suitable place on the south coast for the King to have a healthful and restful holiday to prepare him for the arduous duties of the Silver Jubilee celebrations'.

A few days previously, on 27 February, Queen Mary wrote in her diary: 'an awful night of wind and rain ... it cleared up at three and we drove along the esplanade and then to Beachy Head, a nice drive. Walked in the grounds here and actually picked primroses.' With her lady-in-waiting, Lady Cynthia Colville, she visited the Mint House in Westham and bought some antiques, proving herself to be extremely knowledgeable about her purchases. Afterwards she paid a visit to St. Mary's Church.

Sir James recounted that the royals were delightful visitors and easy to entertain: 'My wife conducted Queen Mary all over our home, displaying our modest family treasurers. Meanwhile King George entrusted himself to me as a separate guide and took a keen sailor's interest in the various gadgets which had been fitted up. When we came to the foot of the narrow, spiral staircase leading to the lantern room, Queen Mary, already aloft, enjoying the stunning views, called down to him, 'George, don't come up here, it's far too steep for you.' To which, His Majesty replied, 'Dammit, I'm coming.' He found the climb a struggle, as, being a heavy smoker, he was plagued by illness, suffering from emphysema, bronchitis, pleurisy and obstructive lung disease.

After his convalescence in Eastbourne, with healthy walks along the promenade to the chalet that the couple used on the western seafront (which now bears a plaque) the King's health improved a little. But after the death of his beloved sister, Princess Victoria, on 3 December 1935, the King started to feel unwell again. Although weak, with a now failing heart, he managed to make his Christmas broadcast 'to my dear people', but he never appeared in public again.

On 20 January 1936 George V took to his bed, and by 9.25pm it became apparent that he was dying. The BBC's Stuart Hibberd announced to the nation that 'The King's life is moving peacefully towards its close.'

Belle Tout –pre WW2.
(Picture courtesy Sue Houlihan.)

THE SECOND WORLD WAR

Troops of Westminster Regiment firing 2-pounder guns on the Shooter's Bottom Range, near Beachy Head.
(Picture courtesy of The Canadian Department of National Defence.)

During the Second World War Belle Tout was left empty, its owners having been evacuated from this vulnerable part of the English coast. Much of the downland was requisitioned by the War Department as a military training ground. Canadian troops came to Britain and were billeted in and around Eastbourne from July 1941 in the run up to D-Day. They took over beach defences on the greater part of the East Sussex coast. Michael Ockenden writes in *Canucks by the Sea – The Canadian Army in Eastbourne during the Second World War* (2nd Edition 2009):

The author must confess to particular admiration for the handful of men around Birling Gap who were responsible for the Beachy Head and Michel Dene Anti-Tank Ranges. The fog and confusion of war, albeit on friendly terrain, and without the horror of direct combat, comes across in the Diary of this unit, which was perched on the Downs from January to July 1943. For the range party, no mascot, no tradition, no glory and no motto – although the latter could well have been 'Doing our best under difficult circumstances'. Strafed by fighter-bombers, knee deep in mud churned up as tanks and self-propelled guns ploughed across the Downland; cursed by artillerymen when firing was halted because of a convoy in the Channel; and up to their elbows in grease as they struggled to unblock drains at the Children's Delight, the pre-war holiday home at Birling Gap which served as a cookhouse for visiting artillery regiments.

Five ranges came under the unit, the largest being the Belle Tout range for 25-pounder guns, where from 1 January 1943 they began firing at a moving target that had been constructed some 200yds east of the lighthouse. In theory the building should have been untouched, being out of the field of fire, but the Canadian troops, blasting away with everything from light howitzers to cannons at wooden silhouettes of tanks suspended on moving cables, hit Belle Tout several times, and a host of shells ended up on the beach.

Michael Ockenden continues:
'The first reference to damage [to Belle Tout] appears in the War diary of the 24th January – 'Two more right angle hits on Belle Tout Lighthouse.' And the following day – 'The score of hits on the Lighthouse has reached thirteen, one on the garage doors.' By the 18th February it was recorded that Belle Tout had been scarred to the tune of 18 hits to date. [This included the loss of the lantern.] 'All accidents, of course.' It didn't help the aims of the gunners that the targets were constantly being blown over by the strong winter winds and men were 'obliged to return to their unit without having fired a shot. And from time to time, a shell would sever the cable which pulled the target trolley, and firing was halted while the range party sent out men to splice it together.'

'In the confined space of the Belle Tout dugout, the car engine pulling the targets overheated. Mechanics had their work cut out to ensure it kept running, and warmer weather made things intolerable. On 15th March it is noted; 'Men punched a hole in the rear of the Belle Tout engine room to keep everyone cool.'

By 1943 daylight could be seen through Belle Tout's shattered 6ft thick walls, and a displaced block can still be seen on the seaward side of the tower.

The CO of the Range Party, Captain Ray Manbert, recorded on 7 June 1943:
I should have mentioned yesterday that Sir James Purves-Stewart, the owner of Belle Tout Lighthouse, came with Lt Col Stevenson of the Army Ordnance Corps to see what damage had been done to his place. I fear he was given a nasty shock, as the building is getting to the point where it will have to be completely re-built. He has asked to have a picture taken and Mr Arch [a local resident and artist] was instructed by me to take one today. The Clerk of Works, Mr Moss and his assistant, Mr Hart, came down to see what damage had been done by the enemy raiders and also to check on our new kitchen stove.

The photograph arrived the next day and was sent to Sir James with a bill for 12s. 6d. Sir James must have made his displeasure felt, as on 24 June there was a visit from officers of South East Command and the War Department Land Agents Office to see what could be done about Sir James Purves-Stewart's lighthouse home. They decided that salvage was useless: the damage was considered total. It was planned to send a truck to pick up anything that Sir James valued. Sir James never returned to live at Belle Tout, dying at his London home on 14 June 1949.
At the end of the war German POWs dismantled the railway that had carried the targets.
In a letter to the *Eastbourne Herald* Barry Earthrowl from Eastbourne states:

Regarding [the article] on World War II shells found at Birling Gap, I must take issue with the last sentence which suggest that Royal Navy warships fired on Beachy Head during WWII for target practice. The static white chalk cliffs are hardly a convincing substitute for swiftly moving grey warships such as the Bismarck or Tirpitz. In fact, the unexploded shells which walkers periodically find at the foot of the cliffs are British anti-tank shells. During the war Canadian gunners trained on a temporary range extending from Belle Tout lighthouse towards Birling Gap. Their guns were sited a little way inland and were trained on moving targets, in the shape of silhouettes of tanks, running along a temporary railway track along the cliff edge.

They were firing a mixture of high explosive shells and armour piercing solid shot rounds and those which failed to hit the targets flew safely over the cliff edge, plunging into the sea or onto the foreshore, depending on the state of the tide.

There was no danger to members of the public at the time because under wartime restrictions the south-east coast was closed and sealed off as part of the anti-invasion precautions. So this is the source of the shells, which are still found to this day.

Unfortunately, some of the Canadian gunners got bored with the intended targets and took pot-shots at Belle Tout lighthouse, which was unoccupied and derelict at the time, causing major damage to the living accommodation on the land side ... If instead this had been a high explosive round, the tower is unlikely to have survived and consequently the post-war restoration may not have taken place and the ruins of Belle Tout may have been allowed to fall into the sea as the cliff edge eroded away. Hopefully, the Canadian gunners put all their training to good use in Normandy in June 1944.

Writing in the *Sussex County Magazine*, James Donne mentioned that he last saw the lighthouse empty but undamaged in the summer of 1941. A few months later everything had changed:

Tanks were skirmishing all along the Downs and about 200 yards east of the Belle Tout a firing range was being constructed. It consisted of a light railway (constructed in the autumn of 1941) crossing the valley formed by two hills, finishing in a deep-dug-out. Inside this was an old car – minus tyres – and the back wheel was used as a winch to tow a life-sized target of a tank along the rails. Soon afterwards firing began, and by 1942, it was incessant from dawn to dusk, never stopping, not even on Sundays. Almost every kind of gun was in use, from cannons to light howitzers, and training crew arrived in relays.

In theory, the lighthouse should have been untouched, being out of the field of fire; in practice we could see the shells bursting around it, and with a telescope, see the deep scars in the masonry from the bursting shrapnel. We were never able to get near it after 1941, but day after day I watched the agony of this famous structure, continually being hit by shells fired wide of the mark. The granite blocks withstood this fierce punishment all through 1942 but by 1943 great rents had appeared in the structure and one could see daylight through the building.

In 1947 Donne chanced to view Belle Tout again while walking over Beachy Head: 'It was shattered from the shells of friendly guns. Had it been Hitler's bombs on a defended building I could have viewed the wreck with the feeling that at least the 'old lady' went down fighting; but the knowledge that this need never have happened sickens me. We have far too few of such famous landmarks left in Sussex today to lose one in such circumstances.'

Another reader, John K. Smith from Dartmouth, recalled in a letter published in 1998 in the Eastbourne Gazette: 'The last time I stood inside the lighthouse it had been reduced to a shell by army gunners. A flat outline of a tank constructed of tubular steel covered with black hessian ran back and forth on a rail below the lighthouse. Anti-tank guns fired across the valley at the moving target. Shots at Belle Tout achieved more spectacular results. As eleven-year-olds we visited the gunnery and infantry training areas. We rarely saw anybody and had the Downs and the military hardware left behind to ourselves.'

Said retired coastguard Garry Russell, BEM:
On the beach off nearby Shooter's Bottom, there laid the remains of an army tank for many years, the result of a mishap where improvements to the tank had added some weight, but no one

June 6 1943

Shattered Belle Tout, 1943.
(Picture courtesy of Sue Houlihan)

had thought about better brakes. It careered off the cliff edge and crashed onto the beach killing all the crew.

Naval ships occasionally turned up to practise shooting at a truck on a set of railway lines situated on the cliff top, guided by signalling instructions. For years afterwards, when we climbed up and down the cliff face, as part of our job, we came across hundred of shells embedded in the chalk.

John Boyle recalls:

From 1953 to 1963 I worked as a student, then solicitor in the office of the Town clerk of Eastbourne, Francis Busby. During that time I had to deal with the grant of a long lease from the County Borough Council to a Mr Cullinan, a London surgeon. I remember that the lessee was building a wall around the lighthouse and was found to have incorporated in the wall a live shell which he had found lying about. This was an unexploded shell resulting from Canadian soldiers using the area as a target range during the war. We called in a bomb disposal team who shut off the area around the lighthouse and recovered many shell cases and some further unexploded shells.

Another visitor to the wrecked building was Mike Peach:

I moved with my parents to Old Town, Eastbourne in 1952. I have memories of cycling to Belle Tout with a school chum. The building was virtually a complete ruin, having been shelled, as I understand it, by the Canadians who had a semi-circular rail track set up in the field the other side of the road. I believe that they ran a gun along the track and fired at Belle Tout to simulate a moving target. Up to a few years ago one could just make out the shelf that the track had been laid on.

My chum and I used to explore the ruins, which, at that time, were a good 50 feet or so away from the cliff edge. I remember jumping down into an empty water cistern (or more likely a cess pit) only to find that I could not reach the rim of the manhole cover to get out. I had to wait while my cycling friend rode back to Eastbourne and summoned my parents to come and haul me out; they then made me walk home because I smelt so badly. (Later in life I was to become a plumber.)

Shattered Belle Tout, (from different angle) 1943.
(Picture courtesy of Sue Houlihan.)

In the very bad winter of 1963, just for fun, I drove my 1934 'Y' Ford car through the substantial snow drifts around Beachy Head and then up the steep service road to Belle Tout, which I believe was then still unoccupied.

In the 1970s I was asked, by a reclusive lady resident, to install a wood burning stove and chimney. By then the building was only 25 feet or so from the cliff edge and I declined the job, telling her that I believed that the stove would suffer from dangerous downdrafts under certain wind conditions.

Julian Martyr from West Dean

recounted a tale from friend David Aston, who as a boy lived in the area during the war: 'He tells that the Canadians gave him and his friends a 'tanner' (six old pence) for any pieces of 'munition' they brought in, live or just the shell cases and a 'bob' (one shilling) for any pieces of plane. Most of the plane pieces were ditched long-range fuel tanks from German bombers returning to France. Either way this was risky to their health!' Julian also recollected that 'There were anti-aircraft batteries here and these were manned by the forces in West Dean. Here at West Dean the Surrey Division of the Quebec Regiment was based, and graffiti suggests that they called themselves the Fighting Hellcats.'

M. Plowright lived by the foot of Beachy Head adjacent to the Pilot Inn from 1923 to 1953, and on a Sunday morning often used to walk up on the Downs past Belle Tout with friends:

In WW2 I served for nearly four years overseas, and in those days, below commissioned ranks you never came back home at all.

An American soldier (in Italy, I think) scrawled on a wall, 'KILROY WAS HERE'. For some reason other soldiers found this cute, and they scrawled 'KILROY WAS HERE' on battered buildings all the way up Italy, and subsequently from Normandy to North Germany. All the troops who served in these areas were familiar with the phrase.

About the end of 1946, and back at home on overseas leave, my mother warned me that Belle Tout had been badly damaged by the Canadian troops. I once again walked up to Beachy Head and on to the lighthouse. Some of the first floor remained and I thought I would climb up on it. I laughed out loud – there on the wall, 'KILROY WAS HERE.'

AFTER THE WAR

1945

Belle Tout 1945.
(Picture courtesy of Sue Houlihan.)

In 1947 a few local councillors, concerned at the demise of this unique building, tried to persuade Eastbourne Corporation to buy it and turn it into a showplace where cream teas could be served in the summer. It was thought that a telescope could be installed, for which a small charge could be made for viewing the Channel. Other ideas mooted were conversion to a youth hostel or a café. One extreme suggestion was to dismantle the lighthouse and sell the stone for building material. But as the cost of purchase and restoration was some £10,000, with no immediate prospect of financial return, the idea was dropped. However, in 1948 Sir James Purves-Stewart, having received £5,000 war compensation, offered the building to 'The Mayor, Aldermen and Burgesses of the county Borough of Eastbourne.' The Deed of Gift was issued on the 13th June 1948. This gesture was marked by a plaque that now stands in the lighthouse area of the Beachy Head Countryside Centre. On 15th August 1949 Belle Tout was designated a Grade II listed building, so any future alterations had to be in character.

Belle Tout, 1947
(Picture by J. Donne from "Sussex County Magazine.")

In a 1949 issue of the *Sussex County Magazine* James Donne wrote:

I notice in the *Eastbourne Gazette* that suggestions are being invited as to what should be done with the old Belle Tout lighthouse. It will be remembered that this historic landmark near Beachy Head was used by Canadian gunners during the war as a target and was so severely shelled that it was left a ruin. The owner, Sir James Purves-Stewart has now given it to Eastbourne Corporation (who owns this part of the Downs) and the question of its future is under discussion. One very interesting suggestion is that it should be rebuilt and opened as a Downland Museum. The writer admits that this would be far from profitable than running it as a café (as has been suggested) but that it would at least be in keeping with the dignity of this famous structure.

THE CULLINANS

Belle Tout, January 1956.
(Picture courtesy Sue Houlihan.)

Although given listed status, Belle Tout remained in a ruinous condition until Dr Edward Revill Cullinan and his wife, Joy, on the 13th April 1956, bought a 90-year lease on the ex-lighthouse at a yearly rental of £15. This included a private roadway on a ¾-acre site. Their application to the council to restore it as a dwelling was unconditionally approved, and they started an extensive rebuilding programme to provide a family home.

The lease states:

[The Lessee] At his own cost to restore Belle Tout in accordance with plans to be approved by the Council carrying out such work of demolition and re-building of the ruins of Belle Tout as may be necessary as to render the ground floor fit for occupation not later than the first day of April One thousand nine hundred and fifty seven, and the first floor fit for habitation not later than the first day of April One thousand nine hundred and fifty eight...

Not to sell or dispose of any earth, chalk, clay, gravel or sand from the demised land or permit the same to be removed nor make any excavation...

To repair and keep in tenable repair the dwelling-house when completed and all additions thereto and all other buildings at any time erected or standing thereon and to keep in good order and repair the approach roadway and to tar and chip with granite chippings the surface thereof, as often as necessary ...

At his own expense to erect a notice board of a type and size and with appropriate lettering to be first approved by the Borough Surveyor at the junction of the main road and the approach road, announcing that the same is a private road and not for public use ...

That the Council shall be under no liability to carry out sea defence works for that part of the beach or cliff adjoining the land hereby demised or for any damage or disturbance caused to the demised land by reason of subsidence land slip or falls of cliff ...

Dr. Cullinan, 1962.
(Picture courtesy Sue Houlihan.)

Dr. Cullinan
(Picture courtesy Sue Houlihan)

Dr Edward Cullinan was a doctor at St. Bartholomew's Hospital. Joy (who's birth name was Dorothea, after the heroine of *Middlemarch*) was the daughter of Thomas Jeeves, Lord Horder of Ashcroft, physician to Edward VIII, George VI and Extra Physician to Queen Elizabeth II. He was also Consulting Physician to the Royal Orthopaedic and Royal Northern Hospitals and Honorary Consulting Physician to the Ministry of Pensions.

The couple brought up four children: Timothy, a doctor, who worked at St Bart's and then in Africa (he died in 2004); Ted, who became a highly successful London architect and designed, among other buildings, the Fountains Abbey Visitor Centre and student residences for the University of East Anglia; Susan; and Anthony (renamed Thomas), who became a Benedictine monk at Ampleforth Abbey. A school friend commented: 'Thomas was a Physicist and mathematician, but had a unique quality of mind, and a constantly fresh way of looking at spiritual and human things.' Susan, Anthony's sister, added: 'He used to bring groups of monks for their summer break to the lighthouse.'

Talking of their purchase of Belle Tout, Joy said: 'Eastbourne had it on their hands for about 10 years after the war. There were always accidents and kids climbing over it. They were on the point of demolishing it.'

The Cullinans attended to the damaged upper storeys and added a new first-floor living area. The remnants of the lantern were dismantled. Ted Cullinan was the designer, and the construction team for the new base was supplied by Walter Llewellyn and Sons Ltd. This company was founded in the early 1900s, and remained family controlled for many years.

Belle Tout, 1970's
(Picture by Mike
Hance, courtesy of
Sue Enoch.)

Belle Tout, 1976.

Pictured L to R
Carr Holland,
Sue Holliday,
Georgiana Bell,
Roger Holmes
and Sue Enoch.

(Picture by Mike
Hance, courtesy
of Sue Enoch.)

L to R.
Georgiana Bell,
Carr Holland,
Sue Holiday,
Joy Cullinan
at Belle Tout
1976.

No lantern room.
Access by a trap
door.

(Picture by Mike
Hance, courtesy of
Sue Enoch.)

Reminiscing in 2006 about the time he spent restoring Belle Tout, Ted Cullinan recounted that he had become friends with Philip Pank, who was an artist 'as well as a natural architect'. They worked together repairing Belle Tout. 'Weekend after weekend and during holidays he used to arrive across the downs in his growling motorbike, and he and I dismantled the granite remains of the upper two floors of the house and built the ground floor with the retained pieces.' He added that they lowered bits of granite down a home-made 100ft long railway track with a 20ft drop from the top to the bottom. 'We used the bigger bits to make a 6ft high boundary wall.' Much of the unused material was stashed just inside the north boundary wall, and was revealed when the bowing wall collapsed in 2008. Belle Tout was finally rebuilt to its original Georgian proportions with a state-of-the-art design.

Urgently in need of a copper dome, Edward Cullinan advertised for a second-hand one. He had a reply from Argentina, offering one of the exact dimensions for nothing. Unfortunately the transport costs came to more than the entire budget for the repair of the lighthouse, so he had to decline the offer.

Dr Edward Cullinan died in 1963, but Joy Cullinan couldn't bear to leave Belle Tout. In 1968 she put in an application to provide bed and breakfast there, but the Eastbourne Downs Preservation and Farms Committee asked the council to defer the request. The committee heard that 'a delegation had met the lessee for the purpose of discussing the proposal, and the lessee had been letting the premises to selected families for certain periods during the summer. The Town Clerk said it would appear that this practice did not require planning permission, but he considered it may be a contravention of the terms of the lease of Belle Tout, which specifically prohibits the use of the premises for anything other than a single dwelling-house.' Mrs Cullinan stated that she hoped to retire in two years' time, to take up permanent residence at Belle Tout and provide bed and breakfast accommodation for walkers. No structural alterations to the premises would be needed. The committee raised no objections to the letting out of the premises to selected families during the summer months, as long as improved safety precautions were taken because of the close proximity of the cliff edge. Permission to use the premises for bed and breakfast accommodation was deferred until June the following year.

Joy and Edward's granddaughter (Ted Cullinan's daughter), Emma Harrington, recalled happy family days at the lighthouse: 'My grandmother was known as 'Granny Lighthouse' because that is where we spent our holidays every summer and Christmas. It was a special place.' She added that her father rebuilt the ground floor, 'then went on a pilgrimage to the church of Ronchamp in France. He returned and built a first floor, heavily influenced by the church's architect Le Corbusier.'

In a 1995 interview for the *Brighton Argus* she said that 'Granny had four children and twelve grandchildren and we all used to cram into the building with its four bedrooms on the ground floor and two in the tower. It is a basic structure, with floors of shiny stone slabs and wood, a million miles from the Hollywood style luxury enjoyed there by Mary Fisher in the BBC's *The Life and Loves of a She-devil*.' She added that her granny slept in a room in the tower that was forbidden to the children, 'which made the tower mysterious'. 'My endearing memory of Granny Lighthouse was of her constantly mowing the lawns, two large ones to the north and the hair-raising one at the cliff's edge. She would march her lawnmower to within 2ft of the 250ft precipice, from which she also used to hurl scraps of food to the waiting seagulls.'

As Emma lay in bed at night she used to hear the wind whistling round the building. She recalled that the swimming pool in the garden (used in the *She-devil* filming) was no more than a slimy pit. They stopped trying to use it when her cousin Phillippa slipped on a water rat that she hadn't seen swimming in its murky depths.

Fresh water hadn't been piped into Belle Tout at that time: 'We would collect drinking water from a tap up the road at Cow Gap, as only sea water came from out of Belle Tout's taps. We got used to this, but unsuspecting visitors would make a cup of tea only to gag loudly at the first sip! We always knew it was a special place, constantly endorsed by the fact that visitors climbed the hill every day to look over the wall. This is a mesmerising place, and the then owners kindly let us all back in for my Granny's 89th birthday. It brought tears to my eyes.'

A Lease of Easement is dated 10 April 1974:

Dorothea Joy Cullinan ... in consideration of the sum of £100 and of the rent hereinafter ... The Trust [the National Trust] hereby demises unto the Lessee full right and liberty to ... lay and thereafter maintain a water pipe one and three-quarter inches in diameter through and under certain land (the property of the Trust) at Birling Gap ... for the purpose of passage and conveyance of water for all reasonable domestic requirements to ... Belle Tout Lighthouse ... To hold the same unto the Lessee from the twenty-fifth day of March One thousand nine hundred and seventy-four for a term of seventy-two years, yielding and paying therefore, if demanded, yearly during the said term the rent of FIVE PENCE to be paid on the First day of January in every year.

A visitor to Belle Tout in the early 1970s was Sue Enoch:

Sue Enoch returns to Belle Tout after 35 years.
(Picture by the author)

'There were various groups from the Institute of Christian Studies, at All Saints' Church, Margaret Street, W1, which stayed in the lighthouse a few times after Joy Cullinan put a flyer through the letterbox advertising Belle Tout as a place where groups could come and study. Our Institute was family orientated and for about 5 years they organised pilgrimages, which used to take place on the Whit Bank Holiday. We set off on the Friday night, and went to places such as Norwich, Canterbury, Chichester, and Winchester. We'd sleep in the church halls, so we would take all the food with us, we could have communion off the back of a tractor, in the open air, then walks to particular points. The church also used to have 'quiet days', done at various centres a little way out of London. Perhaps that was why Belle Tout was chosen, the power of the sea and not being able to control it, it was very spiritual.

'Joy Cullinan was very friendly but quiet. She would often laugh a lot, but she never tried to join in our discussions. She would be in the background, a quiet presence. It was nice to have someone there, like a favourite aunty.

'We got up to the top of the tower, when there was no lantern there, by way of a trap door. At other times we would go for walks across the Seven Sisters cliffs or down to Birling Gap. We usually went to the lighthouse in the winter and there were always roaring fires. Part of our job was to get the driftwood from the beach and bring it back. At first we stayed just at weekend, down on the Friday, back on the Sunday, in groups of about eight to ten people. The first time I saw Belle Tout, I thought it was marvellous; it was so warm inside in spite of the wild winds. I drove down in my car and visited about five times. Mrs. Cullinan did the cooking and we did the washing up. The planning regulations of the then council meant she was not allowed to let out the lighthouse, so she was just paid expenses. It was a fantastic place to stay and after we'd been a few times she felt safe enough to leave us there by ourselves. I am sure near the old entrance there was a wooden cover over an old well. There was no fence on the seaward side, and we were told not to go near the edge. We had a little mantra which I remember that it was 300 feet down to the beach and the lighthouse was 30 feet from the cliff edge. The visits stopped when the Institute closed.

'While we were there we had a knock at the door and a Canadian, probably in his sixties, introduced himself by telling us that he had been in the Canadian Air force during WW2 and had used Belle Tout for target practice. I can remember coming down on the 27th December for the New Year, and one of our group, who was Wagner mad, played music really loud. Suddenly the telephone rang, at which point some wag said, 'That's the neighbours ringing up to complain!'

'We really enjoyed our stays there and I used to read, with some pride, the later stories of its use in TV and films. When I bought my new computer, I was looking for a picture to add as wallpaper and was overjoyed to find a great picture looking across the bay, probably from somewhere past Birling Gap Hotel with Belle Tout on the top of the cliff. I haven't seen Belle Tout close up since the 1970's, and I've always thought fondly of it. The Camden Journal and other local newspapers ran quite a feature on Mrs. Cullinan when she reached her one hundredth birthday. Now it's a B&B I think it might be nice to go and stay there for a weekend.'

Sue Enoch went on to be a teacher and chaperone to children who were working on film sets and stage shows. She has been involved in Grange Hill and most of the Harry Potter films.

Another visitor to Belle Tout in the late 1970s was Dorothy Forsyth, who now lives in Eastbourne. She is an ex-chairperson of the Progressive League (now disbanded), which also had a strong social group:

'Joy Cullinan was a member for many years; we used to have meetings at her house once a month. I'd known Joy for many years, and a group of about eight or ten of us, not representing the Progressive League, just friends in it, would go down to Belle Tout for a few days for about three years running.

'I can remember exactly what it was like inside. Joy, initially, didn't have any running water at the lighthouse: she used to take a couple of containers down to the nearest public toilets at Birling Gap and fill them up with drinking water. Luckily, by the time we were there she had got water laid on. When you went in there on the ground floor, on the left there was a room with about four bed bunks. We used to make up our own beds. Going up some stone steps with a rope rail, there was the bathroom. This was a round room with a cast-iron bath in the middle of the room and one toilet. Then you went up a staircase which didn't have a banister, just another thick rope handrail, through a trap door and you were in a room where you could see all around. On one side there was a lounge with a fireplace for wood burning; on another side, the dining room with a trestle table made by Joy at evening classes, and a hatch to the kitchen, which was open plan and set in the corner of this huge room.

'We used to go with Joy and collect driftwood for the fire from the seashore. It was terrifying because the only access down to the beach was by a rope ladder that swung in the wind. I did wonder whether the rope ever got checked to see if it was fraying. After I'd done this once I decided to stay at the top and be the one to put the wood in the car. I thought it was all a bit dangerous. But we did this because there was this understanding that whatever wood we burnt on the fire we had to replace.

Then you went up the spiral staircase in the tower, where there were, I think, three rooms, one of which Joy used.

'Her father had always pushed her on in life, and she did the same to us. She'd get us to go outside in terrible windy conditions to do things, repairs and such like, although it was mostly the men. One of her favourite invitations was to ask, 'Would you like to come with me for a walk on the beach?' I found the rocks were covered in a black, tar-like substance that was slippery, and if you didn't watch out you could easily be cut off by the incoming tide. Then there was the obstacle of that rope ladder, which frightened me when I climbed it, but some of the party were in their seventies and managed it, so I thought I must do the same. On one occasion a coastguard came up to Joy querying whether it was safe, as the steps were not in use at this time. But she said she had done it many times, and so we proceeded.

In that big lounge we used to have our typical Progressive League activities, such as country dancing, poetry readings and discussions. Also we would get tickets for Glyndebourne to see an opera, take our food with us and we used to put our wine bottle in the lake to keep it cold.

Joy prepared all the food; she wouldn't let anyone help her. We would each pay £3 to stay there with all the food found. I can remember other groups going there, including scouts and birdwatchers.

I watched the BBC series *The Life and Loves of a She-Devil* and wondered what on earth they had done to the building. I couldn't recognise it, it was horrible. I thought it was lovely how Joy had it, and they'd done things for the film. It was nice to stay there; it wasn't cosy, but it was functional. It was often windy outside and you had to hold on, but we just loved staying there, with that lovely big fire. Joy was extremely hardy, fit and independent and she used to walk a lot, and often took us all on rambles. I haven't been back since, not to see the inside, although I've driven by.'

Retired carpenter John Sheppard, from Hailsham, recalled serving a five year apprenticeship with local company Llewellyn as a young man with a first class pass in City and Guilds Certificates. He started with them in 1970 and retired 49 years later. John often worked at Belle Tout, as the company did the bulk of repairs:

'There was a lot of work going on up there, as the joinery department in Eastbourne's Whitley Road, had the job of making a bed for the tower out of Columbian pine, and various other special fittings. They made a lot of circular headed doors. These were made of this Columbian pine, which has quite a distinctive grain with very few knots. If I can remember, the big flat part of the building was a kitchen-cum-lounge, with funny little narrow windows. There was a big worktop, quite modernistic for its time in that particular room.'

Once the main work was finished John was on call to do any smaller jobs, such as re-hanging doors. When he first visited he saw a number of children playing outside, and mistakenly thought they were part of the Cullinan family – but they were children enjoying a seaside holiday.

'I thought to myself, they are very near the edge, and there are so many children there how would they know if one went missing? No-one seemed to be worrying about them, and there was that cliff edge with a 300ft drop.'

Most of the time Belle Tout was empty when he was working there; the Cullinans only used it as a weekend retreat.

John remembered one time in the 1970s when there was an experiment with the clocks, resulting in daylight arriving at around 10 am:

'I happened to be working up there at that time. I rode up on a motor bike; it was pitch dark, no lights, with a swirling morning mist. A colleague who was due to help me said, 'I'm not coming up in that dark, you can go, but I'm not coming there until 10 o'clock.' I went up there as I had a key to the place, and having heard all about a bloke who had broken in and hung himself there, I was a bit wary. I went in and shut the door behind me. It was very creepy: you looked out and there wasn't a single light.

We had a governor, Mr Charles Llewellyn, who used to live at the Queen's Hotel in a suite of rooms. Being in charge of the Small Works Division, he was always in the habit of driving around the various jobs to try and catch blokes out who didn't get to work on time. I thought it unlikely that he would come and check up on me. Then I heard the front door click open, and I was petrified, so I grabbed a hammer and stood behind an inner door. And who should walk in but Charles Llewellyn. He saw me in this distressed state and asked 'Are you all right?' He had driven up there in his old-fashioned Bentley, only to come face to face with me holding this hammer in my hand. I said, 'To be quite honest, sir, I was a bit frightened as I had no idea who was coming in.' He didn't know how close he had come to having his head bashed in.'

On 15 July 1972 Lord Shawcross opened the 80 mile long South Downs Way, which runs from Eastbourne to the Hampshire borders. This is a spectacularly scenic route for walkers and riders, and it passes within yards of Belle Tout, skirting the boundary walls.

Mr G.N. Thompson, General Secretary of the Eastbourne Rambling Club, recalled: 'On Sunday 20th July 1975 Sidney Batt, of Batts the Opticians, Grove Road,

Camden New Journal

Joy for 100 years as the family gather to celebrate a very special birthday

FOUR generations of one family gathered on Saturday to celebrate a very special event – the 100th birthday of Camden Town resident Joy Cullinan.

Joy, whose father Thomas, Lord Horder of Ashford, and late husband Edward were doctors at St Bartholomew's Hospital, is a familiar face in the borough. She worked for the Church Adoption Society in Bloomsbury Square and after retiring in 1980, was a volunteer in the Oxfam shop in Kentish Town Road and CND office in Holloway Road. This week, just days after receiving her telegram from the Queen, she plans to sign up for a poetry class at the Charlie Ratchford centre in Camden Town. But that will come as no surprise to those who know Joy – during her lifetime she has trained in sculpture and social work, once restored a ruined lighthouse on Beachy Head into a family home and was nominated for the New Journal's Pensioner of the Year 20 years ago.

So it was not without a little pride that more than 70 relatives wished her well at the special party in Kentish Town community centre in Busby Place on Saturday. Among the guests were her children Ted, Susan and Anthony, their families and those of her late son Timothy, who was a doctor at St Barts and in Africa, and who died 18 months ago.

Pick of the old-timers!

Joy with her great-grandchildren and above, Joy is nominated for the New Journal's Pensioner of the Year Award in 1985

Camden New Journal, 2005, on Joy's 100th Birthday. (Picture by kind permission of Camden New Journal.)

Eastbourne, took us on a 5 mile family ramble from Beachy Head with a stop at Belle Tout for tea and cakes.' They were all photographed on the top of the lighthouse tower.

Joy Cullinan sold Belle Tout to Lionel and Fay Davidson on the 13th October 1980, and became a volunteer in an Oxfam shop in Kentish Town and in the CND office in the Holloway Road. A few days after receiving her telegram from the Queen in 2005 she celebrated her 100th birthday with a huge family party. The *Camden New Journal* ran a feature on this special event, stating that four generations of her family had gathered together. Included was a photograph of the young Joy standing at the top of Belle Tout's tower. In March 2006 she moved into BUPA's Highgate nursing home, where she died at the age of 103.

Members of the Eastbourne Rambling Club in 1975.
(Picture courtesy of G.N. Thompson.)

THE BELLE TOUT SUICIDE

On 18 October 1967, when the Cullinans were away from Belle Tout, two men smashed a window and broke in. One was later found hanged from the balustrade. At the inquest John Joseph Looney, a penniless 41-year-old Irish labourer, said that he was sitting by the cliff edge when he accepted an invitation from 35-year-old Howard Herbert Robinson, of no fixed address, to join him in getting into the lighthouse. They made cups of tea, and 'We talked and talked for hours about every subject you could think of. He said he had had several businesses, but in each of them, he went down. We went to bed in the same room, but in single beds. Robinson gave me a wrist watch, cufflinks and a cigarette case, saying he wouldn't need them as he had other plans.'

Next morning they both had coffee and admired the beautiful sunrise. Robinson shaved and said, 'Now I am more presentable.' Looney said that he went back to sleep. 'Some sort of noise woke me, I thought maybe the woman of the house had arrived ... then I saw something hanging. I knocked into it. It took me quite a time to realise it was Howard. He looked terrible. I tried to untie the knot, but I couldn't and I couldn't find a knife. Then I heard somebody downstairs.'

JOHN JOSEPH LOONEY

DETECTIVES ARRIVING AT BELLE TOUT
Courtesy Central Library
Eastbourne

The suicide at Belle Tout. Top – John Joseph Looney. Lower- Detectives arriving at Belle Tout.

(Pictures – T.R. Beckett Newspapers, courtesy of East Sussex Library and Information Services.)

This was the cleaner, Mr Cyril Bartlett, of Millbrook Gardens, who said, 'The front door opened easily. I saw a man hanging by the neck from the rail at the top of the stairs. I noticed immediately that his hands were held in front of him, as if tied together. A few seconds later Mr Looney appeared at the top of the stairs. He said, 'Look what's happened, he's hanged himself." Looney finally found a knife, severed the rope and tried to take the weight of the body, but 'his head struck the stairs'. He then cut the rope around Robinson's neck and tried artificial respiration while waiting for the police to arrive.

Mystery surrounds Robinson, who was also known as Howard Robertson, Howard Hilton and Robert Shaw. Inquiries showed that he was married in Eastbourne in 1960 and divorced in 1965. When employed as a manager of K Shoes in London he stole cash and cheques worth some £1,500. In a letter sent to the manager of the company he apologised for the thefts, claiming that he had stomach cancer and was off to spend his final days in the sun.

Robinson went to Jersey, where he obtained employment as a company director with Vogue Styles Ltd, under the name of Howard Hilton Scott, in September 1965. In August 1967 he was interviewed by Jersey police about an alleged insurance fraud concerning a £3,351 claim for damage to clothing owned by the company. He then swiftly departed to Eastbourne, where he stayed in local hotels for a couple of months. At the Birling Gap Hotel he cashed four cheques totalling £5 from a cheque book stolen in Jersey, and finally ran out of funds. Word got round the various hotels about his impecunious situation, leaving him with nowhere to stay.

In a newspaper report, it stated that 'Mrs. Cullinan, owner of Belle Tout, said that the premises had been left secure, and, as it was just used as a weekend home, there was nothing valuable there. A chef, David Aitchison, of Valley des Vaux, Jersey, said that he had shared a flat on the island with a man he knew as Howard Hilton Scott, who had attempted to take his own life with an overdose of aspirin, as he had no money.'

An autopsy revealed no traces of cancer. Although the police initially stated that 'We cannot rule out foul play,' Home Office pathologist Professor Francis Camps said, 'There was nothing inconsistent with the hanging being self-inflicted, and no evidence of manual strangulation.

There is no doubt that this man died pretty rapidly.' A charge alleging Looney was on the premises unlawfully was withdrawn by the police.

LIONEL DAVIDSON

On 13 October 1980 the award-winning author Lionel Davidson and his wife, Fay Davidson, of 23 Carlyle Mansions, Cheyne Walk, London, SW3, took over the lease of Belle Tout from Mrs Cullinan. The Deed of Assignment states: 'The Assignor [Joy Cullinan] has agreed in consideration of the sum of one pound to assign to the Assignees [the Davidsons] the rights and liberties contained in the Lease for all the residue now unexpired of the said term ... It is hereby certified that the transaction hereby effected does not form part of a larger transaction ... of which the amount or value of the consideration exceeds £30,000.'

Born on 31 March 1922, Davidson was the youngest of nine children of an immigrant Jewish tailor. At 14 he left school and went to work as an office boy for the *Spectator* magazine. At 15 he wrote a short story, 'The Ferry', which they published. During the Second World War he joined the Keystone Press Agency as a reporter. As they dealt mainly in photographs he taught himself how to use a camera. At this time he lost 37 relatives at Auschwitz, and when he became a successful writer he refused to let any of his books to be published in Germany. He became a fiction editor for *John Bull* magazine in 1955, and then turned his hand to freelance writing.

On a trip to Europe he had an idea for his debut thriller, *The Night of Wenceslas* (1960). At the time when it was published he had a wife and child, and just £11 in his bank account. This book won him the best first novel award of the Authors' Club and Gold Dagger award. Hollywood producer Hal Wallis bought the film rights to *The Night of Wenceslas* and sold them on to British film producer Betty Box. She turned it into a comedy, *Hot Enough for June* (1964), starring Dirk Bogarde.

Davidson dabbled with writing film scripts, earning some £20,000 a year, but decided that he would 'rather dig roads'. *A Long Way to Shiloh* followed, which became a number one bestseller, winning him another Gold Dagger award. Other titles Davidson wrote were *The Sun Chemist*, described by the *Spectator* as 'the book of the year', *Smith's Gazelle* and *The Chelsea Murders*, which earned him his third Gold Dagger. After a 16-year gap he produced another thriller, *Kolymsky Heights*.

In an interview by Russell James for *Shots* magazine, Davidson was asked, 'What are your true loves?' His reply, 'Curry, whisky and Mozart, preferably in the same evening.'

Davidson bought Belle Tout thinking it would cure him of attacks of writer's block, but he appears never to have moved in, apparently staying at his Conduit Cottage, Heath Street, London, NW3 address.

Pre-purchase enquiries from solicitors Hart, Reade and Co. survive:

The property was wired when built 25 years ago and has not been rewired since ... The vendor does not believe that the access road has been repaired during the tenancy of her late husband and herself. She thinks it may have been last done after the war, in or about 1945. However, the vendor states that the road has been patched from time to time as required and she has never received notice that it requires repair ... The vendor states 'If we leave the front gate open, the public will walk in ... if the front gate is kept shut there is no problem at all.' No doubt the matter could be dealt with by a suitable notice on the gate that this is private property.

Additional enquiries added that 'A survey of the property carried out in March 1980 revealed a geological fault which would eventually cause the lighthouse's collapse ... Having regard to this inherent defect, the lessee's covenants to repair and reinstate ... impose a very onerous liability of the Lessee. The Vendor has apparently received assurances from the Landlord that she would not be responsible for repairs and reinstatement due to this fault and that, when the lighthouse collapses, she will no longer have to pay rates.'

The piped water supply to the lighthouse was tapped into by Eastbourne Borough Council for the purpose of providing water for the downland sheep. But the following terms applied:

1. At your [the Council's] expense, a submeter is installed at the point of tapping and all water consumed is to be paid for quarterly on the usual quarter days.

2. The Council is to indemnify me against any damage caused to the water pipe during tapping or subsequently arising as a direct result of the tapping.

3. This arrangement may continue so long as the Downland pasture improvement programme continues to operate.

4. The Council is to be responsible for all repairs to their submeter and the pipe between it and the trough.

5. Provision should be made to ensure that the route of the South Down Way is kept open at all times.

In 1986, Davidson sold Belle Tout to the BBC. He died on 21 October 2009.

THE LIFE AND LOVES OF A SHE-DEVIL

Application No: .EB/.86 ./. 63 ....

EASTBOURNE BOROUGH COUNCIL
TOWN AND COUNTRY PLANNING ACT, 1971
PERMISSION TO DEVELOP LAND SUBJECT TO CONDITIONS

To: .... BBC. Television, .c/o .Mr.. C. .D'Oyly-John, ...

...... Room .511,. Threshold House, BBC Television Centre, ...

...... Wood. Lane, .LONDON. .W12. 7RJ ....

Situation .... 'BELLE TOUT' LIGHTHOUSE, EASTBOURNE ....

Purpose .. Erection. of. temporary. structures. comprising. scaffolding. around. building. clad. in.

.... feather-edge. board. and. shiplap. timber, .a. glass. canopy/porch. and. a. topping. to. the.

.... existing. tower, .together. with. the. temporary. removal. of. part. of. the. boundary. wall.

In pursuance of their powers under the above Act the council as Local Planning Authority hereby permit you to develop land in accordance with the proposals set out in your application dated ..... 5. February. 1986 ... and shown on the plan(s) submitted therewith, subject to the conditions specified hereunder:—
CONDITIONS

```
          That the temporary structures hereby permitted shall be removed
          and the building and boundary wall reinstated to their former
          condition on or before 30 June 1986 to the satisfaction of the
          Director of Technical Services.
```

The reasons for the Council's decision to grant permission for the development subject to compliance with the conditions set out above are:—
REASONS FOR CONDITIONS

```
          To safeguard the character of this Grade II listed building.
```

This permission is granted subject to the compliance with the Building Regulations, 1985, and general statutory provision in force in the Borough and nothing herein shall be regarded as dispensing with such compliance.

Access for Fire Brigade: Your attention is hereby drawn to the provisions of Section 35 of the East Sussex Act 1981. ~~The Chronically Sick and Disabled Act 1970; also applies please see attached notes.~~

The applicant should read the notes printed on the back of this form.
Copies of the plan(s) and application form are returned herewith.

Dated this .... 12 .... day of .... March .... 19.86 ..

Form T.P.11 Permission conditional.
    Use Class not specified.

DIRECTOR OF TECHNICAL SERVICES

Permission from E.B.C. to erect temporary structure for filming of BBC's The Life and Loves of a She Devil.'
(Document courtesy of David Shaw.)

The lighthouse altered for the BBC drama "The Life and Loves of a She-Devil."
(Picture courtesy of David Wells.)

The BBC purchased Belle Tout for £50,000, to use as a backdrop for a proposed film series, and for a rumoured further £250,000 upgraded the building, including adding a fake lantern room and two windows at ground-floor level on the seaward side.

Belle Tout was one of the main locations for the TV series *The Life and Loves of a She-Devil* (from the 1983 novel by Fay Weldon) starring Patricia Hodge, Dennis Waterman and Julie T. Wallace (who put on 3 stone to play the part). The cast also included Tom Baker, Liz Smith and Miriam Margolyes. This is a tale about a tall and unattractive woman who goes to great lengths to exact revenge on her husband and his beautiful, classy lover, a romantic novelist, who lives in a lighthouse. This drama won four Baftas, with five further nominations. The screenplay was by Ted Whitehead and it was directed by Philip Saville.

Sticking strictly to the script, the BBC transformed the lighthouse into an 'ivory tower', the heroine's love nest, and a large stage set was temporarily added around the building. The work of local landscape gardener David Wells, a former Master Mariner and 1988 winner of the *Sunday Express* Garden of the Year award suitably impressed the BBC TV locations manager Ms Horn when she visited one of his projects, the Eastbourne Butterfly Centre, that he was awarded the contract as landscaper. He said:

'A site meeting was arranged at Belle Tout lighthouse on a bitterly cold day in February. We met the film director, Peter Saville, and producer, Sally Head. I drew up a plan, which was accepted without alterations; it needed a lot of imagination. There was very little plant life surviving; most were laid prostrate owing to the strong winds. There were ivy, elderberry and a brave climbing rose which later produced a fragrant white and pink flower.

Work commenced soon afterwards, and we were to discover that the bitter cold alone would not be the main problem. The force of the wind would hurl pieces of chalk from the cliff face high into the air. On occasions we would retreat to the vans – the hammering on the tin roof could be infernal. Worse was to come; in certain directions the wind would lift sheep droppings – hard pellets that would sting your face and almost blind you. It became a 'hard hat' job.

We used a small digger to shape the site and dig out the 5ft deep swimming pool. One morning, after a night of torrential rain, we returned and found some shiny metal objects that had been scraped by the digger blades. We discovered that they were 5in artillery shells – apparently used by the

Canadian Army during the Second World War for gunnery practice. I informed the police – who informed the bomb squad – who shut the site down. Several sack loads of live shells were u n e a r t h e d , lowered to the beach and d e t o n a t e d . The massive explosion blew seagulls higher than they had p r e v i o u s l y e x p e r i e n c e d !

The Rolls-Royce at the cliff edge.
(Picture courtesy of David Wells.)

The BBC was furious [hold-ups were costly], as so many were made idle. After a day the area was declared safe and the bomb squad departed.

Work progressed to schedule, which included many tons of building materials. It is a sobering thought that the track used by the 22 ton vehicles carrying Ready-Mix cement later disappeared with cliff erosion.

The public showed a great deal of interest in the construction, but were not encouraged – they were easily fobbed off with stories of a future hotel or restaurant. Very convincing when you consider that the mock-up building was held together with scaffolding.

The final landscape included 30 tons of rockery and Sussex stone, a similar amount of gravel, sand, cement, ballast, etc.; also hundreds of bedding plants (petunias, stocks, lobelia and marigolds), rockery alpines, yuccas, cordylines and phormiumss, salt and wind tolerant flowering shrubs

Putting on Belle Tout's temporary lantern by the BBC.
(Picture courtesy of David Wells.)

(viburnum, euonymus, mahonia and philadelphus) and conifers – the latter mature up to 13ft high with large root balls. These were staked and tied against the wind and our work was on schedule in time for filming to commence. We were employed to 'work by' throughout.

I was concerned that the joints in the new turf might show. 'No worries,'

Filming the 'squashed gateaux' scene.
(Picture courtesy of David Wells.)

said director Peter Saville. 'We will blur the shot if necessary. We have even stuck leaves back on a tree to keep summer a bit longer.'

A special fan with 5ft blades and run by a Spitfire engine was brought in from London. This was to provide a gale force effect, but was never used.

Our trees were a bit of a problem on one occasion. With filming from a helicopter above and the resultant down-draught, they wanted to fall over. For the re-take I had them well guyed and was among them, holding on for dear life.

Dozens of BBC TV employees arrived: it appeared that every key player had two assistants. The local parks and gardens superintendent went mad with all the cars parking on the grass. This was special downland grass: it requires sheep grazing and takes years to establish. Eventually the BBC had to supply protective metal plates.

A single toilet in the lighthouse bathroom had to provide for 70 people at times; but the water supply was totally inadequate for the heavy demand and the cistern took an age to fill up. What the public never saw during the filming of the smouldering, passionate bedroom scenes was a filthy, blackened sheepskin rug ... it was the route to the loo!

We were soon to meet Patricia Hodge, Dennis Waterman, Julie Wallace and Tom Baker, and I discovered the lovely Rula Lenska (at that time Dennis Waterman's wife) was knowledgeable about gardening. As I was working she came up and spoke to me. For a brief moment I didn't know who she was, then I said, 'You're Rula Lenska, aren't you?' and we shook hands. To my horror I realised I'd got filthy, muddy hands and had made hers all dirty.

At nearby Birling Gap there was a village of caravans and huts. Here the food was served and everyone, when standing in the queue for tea and cake, was equal!

When filming was going on, total silence was the order: it was amazing where so many people hid. Between every take Patricia Hodge's personal (male) make up artist would attend to her. Filming usually started at about 11am but might go on into the early hours of the morning.

Great effort went into making the story authentic. For example, the white Rolls-Royce provided

Publicity shot. Dennis Waterman
(Bo Bo) and Patricia Hodge
(Mary Fisher.)

by the stunt company ends up teetering on the cliff edge. It was actually controlled by wire cables leading to a winch 50ft away. We had to locate clumps of grass and weeds to hide the cables. The prelude to the 'teeter' was the car being driven along the cliff edge by the drunken mother-in-law, and this scene was carried out by a pretty young stunt woman. Before the shoot she and her boss walked the swerving route and he placed twigs, beyond which it was too dangerous to drive. The route passed through a picnic being enjoyed by Fisher (Hodge), Bo-Bo (Waterman), two children, butler and maid. The production assistants had previously been into Eastbourne and bought a number of chocolate gateaux for the scene – most of them were squashed in re-takes.

A misunderstanding between the director and the props department resulted in the site being 'degraded' by seven years (the period of Bo-Bo's imprisonment). Windows were smashed, graffiti daubed, doors taken off hinges and, for our part, we wrecked the garden and 'blackened' the swimming pool, now filled with flotsam. Bedding plants were pulled out and dumped; the director went bonkers. This all happened on a Sunday, and we had to go out and purchase more identical bedding plants. I cut my own swimming pool cover to fit and to conceal the dirty water.

At the end of Fay Weldon's novel, Mary Fisher was sucked through a window and ended up on the beach below. We heard (not confirmed) that the stunt girl wanted £22,000 for this shot – which required a harness and a catapult. The BBC declined and moved the entire contents of the building 90 degrees so that the girl landed on the grass cliff-top.

We were three to four months working at Belle Tout. When filming was finished the staff took lots of the plants home. Very little of the remaining flora survived the following winter.'

David Wells was also one of the main contractors who supervised dismantling and removal of all the surplus equipment and materials that had been used in the filming. All that was left behind was a pair of ornamental gates that can be seen today at the entrance to the new car park. The tower lantern, a flimsy affair, was taken down and dismantled. Belle Tout's next owner, Paul Foulkes, arranged for it to be taken away, shot-blasted and primed for later re-use.

Coastguard Garry Russell was working in the area when the filming was in progress:

'I actually went inside and where they had built the extension onto the side of the lighthouse, it was like walking into a mansion room; it was absolute luxury, outfitted immaculately with furniture, carpets and curtains.

Whilst we were there in our coastguard capacity, we made arrangements to meet a Navy vehicle just east of Belle Tout. They had a load of ammunition they wanted to get rid of, consisting of 17 5¼in shells stuffed with high explosives, and weighing about 1cwt apiece. We lowered these shells to the beach, and whilst we were doing this the BBC film crew were working on the extension on the side of the lighthouse. I went over to warn them that when the shout went up everyone would have to get back inland. The road was closed east and west; one of the film crew came out with a microphone and hung it over the cliff face to record the explosion; they said they might be able to use it in another film.

I took cover under the rescue trailer, because it was steel, and you heard this enormous thump as this lot went off down on the beach. This, I think, was the charge, which then set off the shells. Then there was on hell of a wallop, the whole of Beachy Head shook and you could hear metal

EASTBOURNE LANDSCAPE GARDENER AWARDED DESIGN CONTRACT FOR THE

BBC TV SERIES
"The Life and Loves of the She Devil"

ON Thursday, 8th October we saw on BBC-2 the start of the bizarre four part series "The Life and Loves of the She Devil", starring Dennis waterman and Patricia Hodges.

The film was made on location in several parts of the country, but the main location was Belle Tout Lighthouse, Eastbourne.

The BBC worked strictly to the script and this involved transforming Belle Tout into an "Ivory Tower" being the heroines love nest. The BBC's own staff erected a temporary building around the old lighthouse. The script also called for a beautiful landscaped garden and swimming pool — Eastbourne landscape gardener Dave Wells was awarded the contract to design and construct the garden and pool out of what was little more than two huge piles of rubble.

Work commenced in the bitterest winter for years and as the dead-line for filming approached it was touch and go for a while. Not only was the weather a problem, but no less than 11 World War II shells were unearthed and these brought work to a stop.

Filming commenced in May and continued for 4 weeks — D. Wells Gardeners being required to be 'on call' throughout. Dave Wells' main worry was that the large imported trees with discreetly hidden nylon guy ropes would not withstand the fierce winds. Returning to Belle Tout now, the wind has done its work and few plants have survived.

DAVE WELLS came to Eastbourne in 1961. At the time he was serving as an officer in the Merchant Navy. In 1970, qualified as a ships' captain, he came ashore to take up an appointment as a Trinity House Pilot, this meant moving to Folkestone. Whilst awaiting a moving date, he started landscape gardening with the kind help of a well known Eastbourne Gardener Ken McCarthy. He found that he enjoyed the life so much that when Trinity House "Called" he took the unprecedented step of turning their offer down. Another interesting project involving Dave Wells was the Eastbourne Butterfly Centre at Royal Parade.

Newspaper cutting courtesy of Eastbourne Herald.

whizzing up in the air and bits of red hot metal were embedding into the road and all around.

I got out from underneath the trailer after about 30 seconds, and this was still going on. You could hear the massive Whoomp and I could see the aftershocks of blast waves in the water going out from the cliff face, it was like a half-circle, and there'd be another Whoomp, which led to another circle, and they were getting bigger the further away they went. Where the explosion had been on the beach, there was an enormous crater, and the cliff face got a good clean.

Then, from the bushes surrounding a nearby farm, we saw two naked women come rushing out. There was red hot metal flying everywhere and they hadn't got a stitch on!'

COASTGUARDS: FILMING AND SAFETY

Garry Russell was again on duty during the 1986 filming of a daring stunt in which a jeep was driven off the cliffs near Belle Tout for the James Bond film *The Living Daylights*. A 17ft Dory, used to recover production equipment from the beach, capsized in the heavy seas and threw three men into the surf. Garry immediately called out the lifeboat. Having made radio contact with Helmsman Ian Stringer and crew-member Derek Tucker, he tried to guide them through a maze of rocks. Once they were within 100yds of the shore, the breaking seas washed the vessel onto a reef. The motor stalled, and Helmsman Stringer had to go over the side and tow the boat to shore, where the engine was tilted up to prevent further damage.

The three men from the Dory were clinging to the upturned boat, and with help from Ian Stringer managed to get it righted. Then coastguard control radioed to warn everyone that a severe squall was approaching. The lifeboat engine re-started, and in spite of 8ft high waves a tow-line was connected to the Dory. But as it moved, heavy seas washed out all the salvaged equipment, the boat stuck on rocks and the tow-line had to be cut. They all headed to the film company's safety launch, *Trinitas*, and the three rescued men were put on board.

For their sterling efforts Helmsman Ian Stringer was awarded the RNLI's bronze medal, the Institution's Thanks on Vellum to crew member Derek Tucker, and a Letter of Thanks, signed by Lieutenant-Commander Brian Miles, Deputy Director of the RNLI, was sent to Coastguard Officer Garry Russell for his help.

Also assisting on this occasion was the safety boat belonging to the Birling Gap Safety Boat Association. This was formed in 1983 after Graham Collins of Birling Gap Hotel was alerted when a man got into difficulties in the seas at Birling Gap. Graham fought his way through the worsening sea conditions (at no small risk to himself) and affected a rescue. For this act he received the Royal Humane Society's Testimonial on Vellum.

As it took some 22 minutes for Eastbourne or Newhaven lifeboats to get to the Birling Gap, a meeting of interested local people decided in December 1983 to form the Safety Boat Association, and made an immediate appeal for funds. The response was tremendous, according to their website:

Almost immediately, it seemed, we were offered a suitable boat and engine by East Dean Motors until we could purchase our own. This was closely followed by Mr Jack Collins of the Birling Gap Hotel offering us the use of a suitable building close to the cliff edge for a boathouse.

Great feats of engineering were wrought in the boathouse, large sections of assorted timber and iron, welding gear and beer were fed in and within a short time we had a launch and recovery gantry to enable the boat to be lowered over the cliff edge.

Throughout the winter of 1983/84, we held jumble sales, coffee mornings, dances, raffles, toy fairs and Sales of Christmas cards to raise funds. We raised enough money to buy essential gear and get started.

The boat was first put into service Easter 1984 while the crew continued to practise their new role on Wednesday evenings. Expert advice and tuition was readily forthcoming from local Lifeboats, regular Coastguards, Pett Level Rescue, St. John Ambulance and many others.

The boat and crew were officially blessed at our Open Day and Fete on the 1st September 1984 and was such a success we decided to hold it annually.

Fund raising continued throughout the winter months and the crew received training on First Aid and radiotelephony.

However, much of what we do goes unnoticed: children on lilos and small inflatables are recovered after being blown out to sea by strong off-shore winds. We help swimmers in trouble, recover persons cut off by the tide, assist the Coastguard and Lifeboat and search for missing persons. We give first aid to visitors (dogs as well) that slip on the rocks, etc. And we assisted as Safety Boat for the film *The Life and Loves of a She-Devil*.

In the film *Piece of Cake* some of the crew even took part and we had our boat standing by on a number of occasions during the filming.

Involvement in various filming occasions boosted the Association's funds, enabling them to purchase their own engine, and with collections made by the late Miss Florence Whittaker of Birling Gap Hotel they were able to buy their own boat.

David Cranstone, an ex-coastguard and now actively involved with the Safety Boat, has said that when their services were required a crew of two went out in the boat, checking in by radio on Marine Channel 16 every 15 minutes to a team of volunteers on the beach.

As Second World War shells were constantly being dug up, or revealed after cliff falls, the Army disposal team often had to be called in and ferried along to the beach below Belle Tout. The shells were exploded on the shore, after all parties had been warned of the dangers. David Cranstone recalled: 'We would tell them on top to take cover as there was going to be a bit of a big bang ... We heard that one of the Arms Disposal Team was approached by an irate gentleman who complained that a piece of shrapnel had whizzed over his wife's head. Afterwards a joker in the team commented, 'What's he complaining about? We didn't hit her."

PAUL AND SHIRLEY FOULKES

The late Paul Foulkes at Belle Tout.
(Picture by Bob Fountain.)

Belle Tout was put up for sale again, and bought on the 7th July 1986, as a weekend retreat by Paul Colwyn and Shirley Foulkes, of 16 St. Paul's Place, London, N1. Asked by a journalist 'What, for you, was the attraction of this remote, dumpy, 47 foot high building that became redundant as a working lighthouse many years ago?' Shirley Foulkes replied, 'Take a good look around you. That's why we bought it.' From the elevated position of the restored tower balcony, 334ft above sea level, she pointed out the views, which she described as 'a feast for the eyes':

'To the west you can see the remains of a Bronze Age settlement, and the green trimmed undulations of the famous Seven Sisters chalk cliffs stretching along the coast to Seaford Head. Eastwards, the 500 foot high headland of Beachy Head towers over the red and white striped column of the Beachy Head lighthouse. Northwards, there are Kipling's whale-backed downs, and seawards, 30 miles of uninterrupted views across the English Channel. The only sounds we hear are the gentle splashing of waves on the beach far below and the songs of skylarks mingling with the mewing of gulls. Apart from walkers on the well-trodden adjacent South Downs Way, the only other neighbours we have are rabbits and sheep, and according to local legend, the odd ghost or two.'

Mr. and Mrs. Foulkes continued with the restoration of Belle Tout, sympathetically keeping the maritime feel of the building. Pictures of sailing ships were hung on many of the walls, and there were thick rope handrails on the stone stairways. The four bedrooms on the ground floor were reminiscent of ships' cabins, and wood was used for the fitted wardrobes and floors. Also on the ground floor was a most unusual circular bathroom 11ft in diameter, which had a cast-iron bath in a centrally raised position. On the first floor the light and spacious 36ft by 21ft reception room with an olive wood floor gave spectacular views of the Downs and the sea. Numerous shelves were filled with artefacts washed up on the beach from past shipwrecks. Shirley said, 'We go down to Birling Gap and can usually find something of interest on the shore.' Tucked away in one corner the compact, fully fitted kitchen with a quarry tiled floor was equipped with a built-in electric oven and hob.

Narrow winding steps led to the top of the lighthouse tower. Halfway up there was a small room where it was believed oil for the lamps had been kept. It was converted into a small bedroom with a wall bunk, and proved a popular sleeping place when Paul and Shirley's grandchildren came to visit.

At the top of the tower they decided, in 1988, to reinstate the refurbished 16½ft diameter lantern used by the BBC. It took a large crane to get it lowered into position inside the balcony railings. As the lantern would no longer be used to guide ships, they fitted the interior out with comfortable furniture. Residents and visitors could sit and relax, admiring the magnificent panorama.

By 1995 Mr. and Mrs. Foulkes decided that, because of the relocation of their business, resulting in long periods of travel between work and home, Belle Tout would have to be sold. Shirley said, 'I very much hope whoever buys it will continue to use it as a real family home.'

Handling the sale was Darren Jacques at the Cornfield Road, Eastbourne, branch of estate agents Fox and Sons. According to the sales description, for an asking price of £350,000 a buyer would get '4 double bedrooms, open plan living area with olive wood floor, 2 garages and walled garden'.

The restored lantern room.
(Picture by Bob Fountain.)

A new lantern room/sun lounge about to be placed on top of the old Belle Tout lighthouse, June 1988 {Beckett Newspapers}

Replacing the restored lantern room in 1988.
(Picture courtesy of T.R. Beckett Newspapers.)

BELLE TOUT LIGHTHOUSE
Historic landmark in elevated position along cliffs at Beachy Head. Outstanding views. Lower half of Beachy Head Lighthouse dating back to 1831. 4 beds, 36ft rec rm, circular bath, 2 small tower rms, tower observation rm. 2 gges. Grounds.
PRICE ON APPLICATION

Belle Tout advertised for sale in 1994.
(Picture courtesy of T.R. Beckett Newspapers.)

THE ROBERTS FAMILY

From "The Mail on Sunday."
(Picture by kind permission of The Mail on Sunday.)

Louise Anita Roberts took over the lease of Belle Tout for a rumoured £200,000. When she and her husband, Australian born Mark Roberts, walked into the estate agents they said, 'We're looking for a house. What have you got near Beachy Head?' They instantly fell in love with Belle Tout. 'It was worth it ... although a lot of people said we were mad. It has been a lot of hard work, probably more than we thought, especially the last few months ... we had to make a commitment and we felt there was a special attraction about the place, so we grabbed at it. It is like being in the middle of nowhere. We don't have a television, although we do have electricity.'

On 13 August 1998 they were granted permission to 'Use two double bedrooms for bed and breakfast accommodation'.

However, after a number of substantial cliff falls nearby, caused by ongoing coastal erosion, it became evident that Belle Tout was soon going to end up on the beach, 285ft below.

The chalk cliffs were formed over 30 million years ago, made up from the shells of billions of microscopic planktonic algae that hardened into the white rock we see today. High tides and the tremendous force of the waves wear away the base of the cliffs and inroads are made into the chalk base until it can no longer support the upper part, which eventually tumbles down to the beach.

To preserve the value of the landscape, one of the pivotal conditions of the management of the Heritage Coast is that it is left undeveloped, which means that no sea defences can be built even though the cliffs are receding at an estimated average of about 3ft a year. With global warming and sea levels rising, the rate of erosion is expected to increase – and in January 1999 an area 55ft x 230ft broke off and fell to the beach.

Consulting Civil and Structural Engineers, Tribrach Associates, stated that:

The only way of assessing the likely future erosion is by studying the rate of erosion that has occurred in the past. Records in Mrs Roberts' possession show that in 1896 the distance from the front of the turret to the cliff edge was 70 feet. The present dimension is 24 feet. A total of 46 feet of cliff has disappeared

Advert. Open Days at Belle Tout.
(Picture courtesy of T.R. Beckett Newspapers.)

Belle Tout Lighthouse
Beachy Head East Sussex BN20 0AE

Mr L. B. Dennis
C/o 172 Percival Road
Hampden Park
BN22 9JU

Thursday, 10 December 1998

Dear Mr L. B. Dennis,

Please find enclosed your Certificate of Appreciation to mark your kind support towards saving Belle Tout Lighthouse.

All those who have supported the project by *"buying a brick"* will be noted in a role of honour to be printed in the Eastbourne Herald from this week as part of the general weekly update on progress with the works.

We will be writing to you again when we will send out a Belle Tout Newsletter and of course to give details of the exciting day Belle Tout actually moves.

By 'buying a brick' you have enabled this project to begin in earnest. Recent cliff falls have meant we do need to move the building as soon as possible. It is only with the financial help and indeed encouragement your support gives us that we are able to draw together the team of specialists and research compiled over the past two years to start the work to save this prominent local landmark.

If you would like any further information please do not hesitate to contact us at Belle Tout Lighthouse on (01323) 423 520

Once again thankyou for your support.

Sincerely,

Sheila Charlton

Sheila Charlton
The Southdowns Lighthouse Trust

PS If the details on the certificate are incorrect please do not hesitate to contact me and a new correct certificate will be issued.

Letter of Appreciation. Supporting 'Buy a Brick.'
(Courtesy of Chas Bell.)

in the past 102 years; an average of 0.46 feet/year ... [if] the lighthouse is to be moved and re-sited 17m to the north of its present position, taking account of the previous rate of erosion, it could be in the order of 120 years before the extra area of cliff is lost.

Was it therefore possible for the building to be moved back from the cliff edge? It appeared this was technically possible, at a probable cost of £250,000. Therefore planning permission was sought in November 1997 to move 'the lighthouse (tower and house) by underpinning, jacking and sliding to a new position 17 metres north of present position plus new storey and lower ground level', as nature seemed to be issuing a 'move it or lose it' ultimatum. In February 1998 this plan was approved.

A bid was submitted for £140,000 lottery cash, with Belle Tout just yards from the edge. To raise the extra money, the Roberts family opened their unique home to interested visitors for two days in September as part of the Heritage Open Days, selling tickets costing £5.50 (£5 to the lighthouse fund, 50p for administration costs). This was so successful that other Open Days were arranged. Mr Roberts said, 'Every open weekend has been a total success. All the tickets went, and people without still came up to Belle Tout, standing by the gates in the hope they could get in. But, unfortunately, we can only have limited numbers.' Over one successful weekend, 400 tickets were sold from the Cornfield Road Information Centre. Each purchaser was given a time slot to prevent overcrowding, and visitors were given guided tours, with the opportunity to take photographs.

The Southdown Lighthouse Trust was set up to raise funds, and Mark Roberts (at that time a councillor) was quoted in the local press: 'The plans have now got to an exciting and very vital stage. Belle Tout is a unique building and the move has attracted interest from all over the world. We sincerely hope the Lottery Fund will look favourably on our application.'

In July the lottery grant was refused: 'There are major aspects of the proposal which do not square with our priorities or our main assessment criteria.' Constrained by a shortage of cash and by red tape, the move seemed doomed. A further fund-raising campaign was set up, the Save Belle Tout Lighthouse Appeal. Supporters were urged to buy a brick from between £10 to £60 and 'play a crucial part in saving the lighthouse and become part of the history of Belle Tout'. Everyone who contributed was to have their name inscribed on a plaque that would be erected at the relocated lighthouse – 'recognising the essential role that the people of Eastbourne have played. Every person or company that bought a brick is guaranteed a mention in a Roll of Honour that would be printed in the *Eastbourne Herald* each week, plus a mention on local radio.' In addition to this every contributor would get an entry

Certificate of Appreciation. Supporting 'Buy a Brick.'
(Courtesy of Chas Bell.)

ticket to watch the moving of the lighthouse. Companies were encouraged to contribute to 'a massive time capsule that will be buried at the time of the move and dug up 100 years after the date of the move, unless it is unearthed earlier by cliff erosion'. Additionally, companies contributing £50 would receive an invitation to a reunion in 2000. Other suggested options were invitations to businesses for their employees to come to the moving and open days, enjoy dinner at the lighthouse whilst watching the sunset, all for the equivalent cost of hiring facilities in a hotel. Belle Tout could also be available to hire for product launches, corporate training or filming.

One supporter was Chas Bell, from Hampden Park, Eastbourne, who donated £10 towards the Buy a Brick campaign. For this he got a smart certificate, a letter of acknowledgement from Mark Roberts, an invitation to a conducted tour of Belle Tout on Saturday 21 November at 3.30pm, and a special pass to allow him to watch the historic move from the cliff edge in March the following year. Chas's donation was gifted in memory of his father-in-law, Lionel Dennis, whose name went on the Roll of Honour.

The ambitious move had the full backing of Eastbourne Borough Council. Councillor Brian Whitby said, 'This must be one of the most unusual planning applications ever to come to this committee. It is an important landmark and hundreds and thousands of people come to visit it every year.' 'It is a very courageous and worthwhile scheme,' said committee chairman Maurice Skilton. 'It is a significant building. We must save it for future generations. These people deserve all the support.'

The then Worshipful the Mayor of Eastbourne, Councillor Beryl Healey, also supported the move:
The famous Beachy Head area has two unique lighthouses which attract thousands of visitors to the area annually. There is the Beachy Head light, located on a small landmass in the ocean at the bottom of the cliffs, and the more historic Belle Tout, built in 1834, which is currently situated precariously on the chalk cliff edge above. Often, bad weather restricts the view of the Beachy Head light, and the only lighthouse that can be seen by visitors is Belle Tout.

This crowning landmark on Eastbourne's downland has had a chequered history – abandoned, derelict, used for 'friendly fire' target practice during WWII, lovingly restored and made famous as a film site. Once 100ft from the cliff edge, breakaway chalk has, over the years, brought the lighthouse to its current position within just 30ft of the edge and into a position of danger of plunging into the sea

Application No. EB/97/0629

EASTBOURNE BOROUGH COUNCIL

TOWN AND COUNTRY PLANNING ACT 1990

PERMISSION TO DEVELOP LAND SUBJECT TO CONDITIONS

To: Mr. and Mrs. M. Roberts
c/o Dominic Cullinan Architecture
4th Floor
5 Great Sutton Street
LONDON
EC1V 0BX

Location: BELLE TOUT LIGHTHOUSE, BEACHY HEAD, EASTBOURNE

Proposal: To move the existing lighthouse (tower and house) by underpinning, jacking and sliding to a new position 17 metres north of present position plus new storey at lower ground level.

In pursuance of their powers under the above Act, the Council as Local Planning Authority hereby permit you to develop land in accordance with the proposals set out in your application dated 24 November 1997 and shown on the plan(s) submitted therewith, subject to the conditions as specified hereunder:-

CONDITIONS

SEE SCHEDULE OF CONDITIONS ATTACHED

The reasons for the Council's decision to grant permission for the development subject to compliance with the conditions set out above are:-

REASONS FOR CONDITIONS

SEE SCHEDULE OF REASONS FOR CONDITIONS ATTACHED

This permission must not be treated as an approval under the Building Regulations and is granted subject to due compliance with the general statutory provisions in force in the Borough and nothing herein shall be regarded as dispensing with such compliance.

Access for Fire Brigade: your attention is hereby drawn to the provisions of Section 35 of the East Sussex Act 1981.

Copies of the plan(s) and application form are returned herewith.

Dated this 24 day of February 1998

Head of Planning

The applicant should read the notes printed on the back of this form.

Copy of Planning Application to move Belle Tout away from the cliff edge.
(Courtesy of David Shaw.)

Eastbourne Herald, Friday, September 11, 1998 5

Sept 125/20

CIVIC leaders and guests outside Belle Tout before the Duke cuts the first sod to launch the ambitious project to move the lighthouse back 50ft from the edge.

Pictures:
Andy
Butler

Sept 125/23

THE DUKE digs the first piece of turf to launch the project.

Sept 125/15

signing the visitor's book.

Visit by the Duke of Gloucester in 1998.
(Pictures by Andy Butler. Courtesy T.R. Beckett Newspapers.)

below. Situated near Horseshoe Plantation which is famous for its rare migrating birds and endangered British orchids, the elevated Belle Tout has a unique character which needs to be saved and sustained.

As Mayor of Eastbourne, I am delighted that this historic building will remain as part of Eastbourne's heritage for future generations to visit and enjoy and I look forward to seeing the migration of this building to a safer base away from the crumbling cliff edge. This brave project must be supported – not only by Eastbourne people but by the thousands who visit the area.

Mark Roberts was encouraged by the results:

After a number of discussions with Eastbourne Borough Council we are pleased to announce that all outstanding issues have been resolved and we will be commencing with the archaeological survey on November 16th. Although we do still require more funding we are committed to starting the work as soon as possible. The plans to save Belle Tout have required careful consideration over the past 18 months. With the continued advice from the council officers and members we now have a strong project which will preserve this lighthouse and its history for many generations. Eastbourne Borough Council, both officers and councillors, have been tremendously supportive throughout the course of this planning application and I would like to pay tribute to their hard work and dedication. It would be absolutely devastating for the town to lose this building that has played such an intrinsic role in the past.

Eastbourne builders were asked to submit tenders for the work. As Mark Roberts said, 'We are very keen for this work to be carried out by a local company.'

Abbey Pynford (now Abbey Pynford Foundation Systems) secured the contract, and preliminary design work began in 1997.

It was explained that the project would be split into separate stages. First there was the excavation of the current and new site. Second there was the underpinning of the lighthouse, preparing it for its move. The third stage involved a specialist contractor pushing or pulling the building along tracks to its new position. The move was horizontal, so that the building's eventual altitude would remain the same. To accommodate the steep fall of the garden, a new base was to be built onto the lighthouse.

The top priority was devising a way of moving the structure without putting any significant

Downland Rambles.
(Tour ticket picture courtesy of Chas Bell.)

horizontal loads into the ground close to the cliff face. There was the possibility that any attempt to jack the building northwards would just push the cliff face southwards into the sea.

In September 1998 the Duke of Gloucester was the honoured guest as the ambitious plans to move the endangered building were officially launched. In near gale force winds he was welcomed by Maurice Skilton, East Sussex County Council Chairman, Eastbourne Mayor Beryl Healey and Sari Conway, Eastbourne Borough Council chief executive.

The duke cut into a piece of turf, as part of an archaeological dig to make sure the move would not disturb any historic remains. Afterwards he chatted to architects and engineers who were involved in the move. At the end of his visit the duke signed the visitors' book in the lantern room and was presented with a model of the lighthouse by Louise Roberts. He stayed for about 45 minutes, having been given a guided tour and a brief talk on the history of Belle Tout by Mr Roberts, who said afterwards, 'I think it all went extremely well. The duke really enjoyed his visit and he didn't want to go. Hopefully we will have another royal visitor on the day of the move.'

In December 1998, after the Roberts family had moved into temporary accommodation, thieves

Thank you for making a confirmed booking on

SATURDAY 21st of November 1998 at 3:30pm.

The Belle Tout Lighthouse Tour

"Belle Tout Lighthouse stands proudly on the cliff top of Beachy Head. Its rich and varied history was, until now, kept firmly within the solid granite walls. Despite being given to the people of Eastbourne after the Second World War, Belle Tout remains a mystery. This is the third time Belle Tout has been officially open to the public ever and many people who have lived locally all their lives know nothing of their famous landmark's history."

Please note due to demand you can only be admitted at the time specified, each tour will last 20min.

All proceeds are going to the South Downs Lighthouse Trust which is a charity working to save the Lighthouse for future generations.

© Copyright - The South Downs Lighthouse Trust October 1998

Souvenir ticket price £5.00
Additional booking fee 50p

Belle Tout lighthouse tour ticket.
(Copy courtesy of Chas Bell.)

stole equipment from the Belle Tout building site. Abbey Pynford's office was broken into and two hard hats, a luminous jacket and a West Ham chequered jacket were stolen. Mark Roberts warned light-fingered criminals to stay away from the site: 'There is nothing in the lighthouse at all – it has all been removed. And the workmen are up there every day.'

That same month Abbey Pynford started with a conventional underpinning job. 'Sacrificial steel stools' were slotted under the load-bearing walls, then reinforced concrete beams were cast between and around them. Extra beams linked the wall support beams to create a stiff load-bearing grillage. Beneath this, some 13ft below original ground level, the contractor created four massive, heavily reinforced, north/south 'slide beams'.

Mr Roberts said: 'There is not much to see at the moment because they are working from the inside out. They have taken up all the flooring and in some places dug trenches 10ft deep. There are steel cages laid in the trenches to reinforce the building and one metre wide railway tracks are in the process of being put down so the building can slide away from the cliff edge.'

From *Cranes Today* magazine there was a feature about the moving of Belle Tout:

A new single storey basement structure, or reception box, had already been prepared on the former croquet lawn to the exact plan of the existing structure. All that remained to do was move the lighthouse onto these new foundations, 17m to the north.

To do this, the engineers cast a reinforced concrete ring beam under the structure's load-bearing walls and installed four concrete slide track beams, tied into the reception box and extending out beneath the ring beam. These track beams became part of the jacking structure as well as providing the rails for the lighthouse to move on. To lift the 850 ton lighthouse, Abbey Pynford used single action hydraulic jacks, each with a lifting capacity of 60t.

All the jacks were linked into the same hydraulic circuit and there were a series of 10 extensometers attached around the perimeter of the lighthouse to monitor and differential movements. Monitoring was done with Abbey Pynford's Equilift computer system, which used information fed back by the extensometers to control the movement of the jacks. Once the lighthouse was jacked up, mechanical screw props were placed under the ring beam to support the structure while the lifting jacks were inverted and fixed to the ring beam.

Now fitted with grease skates on their underside, the jacks were extended again until the grease skates rested on the steel rails attached to the slide beams.

Much speculation had focused on whether the pushing force of the jacks would be too great for the fractured chalk of the cliff edge, initiating a disastrous rock fall. 'In fact, the force needed to move the lighthouse was actually quite small,' a spokesperson said. 'The skates are extremely efficient, and it needed only about 5 per cent of the vertical load to get the lighthouse moving. This equated to about 40t to overcome inertia, falling to 20t to continue to travel along the rails. We needed to control the jacks to slow the movement as well as start it. If there had been a strong southerly blowing off the English Channel, we might not have needed any jacks at all, except we wouldn't have been able to stop it moving.'

By 8 January 1999 eight workmen from Abbey Pynford were working seven days a week to ensure that the lighthouse move could go ahead on schedule. They dug down deep into the foundations, creating openings and tunnels under the outer walls. As the lighthouse may well need moving again in the next 30 to 50 years, all the specialist beam work has been left in place.

At the end of January Louise Roberts had a production of her own – a new baby brother, Quinn, for 11-month-old Haven. Louise said that Haven was getting on fine with the new arrival as 'She's too young to be jealous. And there is something special about having a girl and a boy – although we haven't had much sleep.'

Then a massive cliff fall took away the front garden, making the need to move Belle Tout as quickly as possible even more urgent. Mark Roberts said:

'There was this massive rumbling, like thunder, the tower started to gently move and we just grabbed the baby and the dog, jumped into the car and drove down the hill. We sat there for about ten minutes not knowing what to expect. There was so much dust in the air that we could not see if Belle Tout was still standing. When it cleared, we discovered that we had escaped narrowly. This is very worrying because it suggests that the cliffs are going through an active cycle of erosion. Hopefully, we have started the work at Belle Tout just in time. I wouldn't like to wait another winter. We are definitely up against the clock. If we do not move it, it will move of its own accord. This is a war with Mother Nature and we have got to take action if we are going to win.'

Mr Roberts warned walkers not to let their curiosity get the better of them: 'Don't go up to the edge to get a better look at the cliff fall. We don't know if the ground there is structurally sound.' Louise Roberts added: 'One moment you look out and you can see 40ft of your garden. Then there's a rumble and all you can see is 10 ft.'

Abbey Pynford's Head of Special Contracts said that the force of the sea pounding against the cliffs below Belle Tout could trigger another landslide at any time, possibly carrying the lighthouse with it into the sea:

'The erosion of the cliff has accelerated rapidly in the past few years, but nobody knows for sure when it will next go and nature is a terrible boss.

Workmen have been carefully digging underneath the lighthouse, underpinning the foundations and a framework of reinforced concrete beams have been placed under all the load-bearing walls. We have taken the building apart bit by bit, like a jigsaw puzzle, stripping it to its bare structure before we push it down the hill. We are not fixing it permanently so future occupiers will be able to move it further down the hill when it becomes necessary.'

One week later unexploded war shells were discovered washed up on the beach below the lighthouse. Owing to the high tide a bomb disposal squad was unable to act immediately to remove them. Mark Roberts faced an anxious wait while the danger could be assessed: 'I couldn't believe it when the coastguard suggested that there might have to be a controlled explosion. I don't need this. Any explosion could spark another rock fall at Beachy Head.'

French-born Eric Greber, from Professional Property Services, was acting as a consultant to the project. Belle Tout held a special interest for him as his father had painted a number of scenes around the area. He said, 'We are hoping to find a painting of the lighthouse that my father has done, which would be lovely.' He added jokingly, referring to the problems of unexploded shells and falling cliffs, 'Maybe it takes a Frenchman and an Australian to save a piece of British heritage.'

Eastbourne-based Tim Cobb Associates helped the Roberts' handle the overwhelming media interest in the move. 'They are giving us general advice on associated issues. Tim and his wife Sue are both journalists and so understand the needs of the media ... explaining to them in simple terms what is happening ... They will be helping the journalists get the information and film footage they require, while at the same time ensuring the media does not hinder or endanger the process.'

Camera crews flew in from many countries around the world, including France, Germany and Japan. ITN, Channel 5, Sky News and BBC's 24-hour news service were joined by Meridian, South Today, Southern Counties Radio and Southern FM, as well as newspaper journalists from *The Times*, *Daily Mail* and *Independent*.

One of the TV presenters, Craig Doyle, said, 'Basically, this has got everything. You've got a crumbling cliff edge and the human interest with the family living there. It's got all the drama ... The mechanics involved are incredible – it is boys and their toys.'

Bad weather delayed the lighthouse move from 9 March 1999 for a week. All the emergency services were on stand-by to cope if anything went wrong. There had been months of planning, and a disaster management headquarters was set up at the nearby Countryside Centre.

Ron Cussons, Eastbourne's director of Tourism, Leisure and Amenities said:

'We have consulted with the Coastguard, Fire Brigade, Police, Ambulance Service and others. We have investigated every emergency that may have occurred. We have got three radio systems in case the land lines go down. A special aerial had to be erected. In these situations communications are the key.

The best place to watch this event is in the comfort of your own home via the regular television news updates. Anybody who wants to get to Belle Tout to see the move first hand should be aware that it will be a difficult journey with a lot of walking involved. The road closures and restrictions are not aimed at stopping the enjoyment and participation of the public. They are to ensure that emergency services can gain access and exit at all times.'

Relocation date 17th March 1999

Pick up time from Beachy Head Roadblock
~~2.30~~ 4.00 pm
Please note for safety reasons access will only be granted at the specified time

This pass will admit ONE person to Belle Tout Lighthouse
Please proceed just beyond the roadblock at Beachy Head and show this pass to the uniformed Young Engineer Stewards

Copy of ticket to the moving of Belle Tout.
(Courtesy of Chas Bell.)

The road was closed from the Beachy Head pub to Birling Gap: 'in the event of traffic congestion either end, further sections of this road may be closed to ensure access at all times for emergency services.' Beach access to the site via Birling Gap and Cow Gap was blocked, spectators being advised by signpost 'to walk around the base of the cliffs from the Eastbourne beach access point'. Drivers were strongly advised not to bring their cars to the area, while 'Viewing the move from the east side of the lighthouse is not recommended due to the instability of the cliff top area. Much of this section has already been cordoned off.'

To cater for the hundreds of people wanting to visit the site with no transport, buses ran from the Congress Theatre up to the road block just beyond the Beachy Head pub. Tickets costs £3.50 return. A shuttle bus was provided to Belle Tout, costing £1 each way.

During the move the Fire Brigade's heavy rescue team stood by, in case the building collapsed onto any of the workers beneath. Eastbourne Station Officer Adrian White pointed out that there is always a small risk in moving a structure of this size. 'The heavy rescue team has air bags which can each lift 60 tonnes.'

On Wednesday 17 March 1999 – the day of the move – the weather was perfect. Many groups of picnickers were enjoying the atmosphere, sitting among the hundreds of sightseers who had come from all around the world to watch an impossible dream come true. Louise Roberts said, 'I turned 30 just a couple of days ago and this is the perfect birthday present. It is going to be a bit nerve-wracking watching the lighthouse move, but a lot less worrying than if it fell into the sea.' Having given birth to her son just six weeks earlier, 'You could say it all came at once for us. It will be a great relief when we get back to normal.'

A very special guest was 93-year-old Dorothea (Joy) Cullinan, who had lived with her family at Belle Tout from 1956 to 1980 and had been specially invited to get the move under way. She was quoted in the *Eastbourne Herald*. 'This may never have come about if it hadn't been for my family who bought the building and developed it.' Joining her were 15 of her family. Granddaughter Joanna Owen recalled her childhood visits to Belle Tout: 'We used to come over on school holidays and have a great time up there. On one occasion, in 1975, we couldn't find my grandmother, and when we started looking for her we found that she had climbed a little way down the cliffs and was plugging the rabbit holes with cement. She was worried that their burrowing would weaken the cliff.'

At 9.25am Joy Cullinan pressed the switch for the hydraulic pump to start and, aided by a theatrical push from an obliging workman, the lighthouse slowly began to edge towards its new location. Ensuring the lift was perfectly balanced was a major challenge. A spokesperson for Abbey Pynford said, 'There's always a tendency for structures to lift in sections. Our jacks are fitted with

The
Belle Tout
lighthouse...

...Back from
the brink

ABBEY PYNFORD PLC

Moving Belle Tout. Abbey Pynford literature.
(Courtesy of Abbey Pynford)

rheostats and monitored by computer, so we can adjust individual jacks to keep everything on an even keel.'

The ultimate purpose of the lift was to create space for the installation of the company's specially adapted 'grease skates' and inverted jacks. Before this could happen, precast concrete 'cheeses' were inserted between the building and the slide beams until the contractor was ready to start the slide. They 'don't like to be static under load for long, they begin to seize up, [so] we inserted the cheeses and lowered the building back down onto these for a week.'

The interval was used to fix 3mm steel plate slide surfaces to the tops of the slide beams, which had to be constructed to very tight tolerances. The contractor calculated that a lateral force of 85 tons would be needed to overcome Belle Tout's inertia – but once the building was moving on a cushion of grease a force of less than 20 tons would suffice; a figure perilously close to the total calculated wind load produced by a southerly gale:

From the point of view of a south wind, the turret is 90m high; in those circumstances the pushing

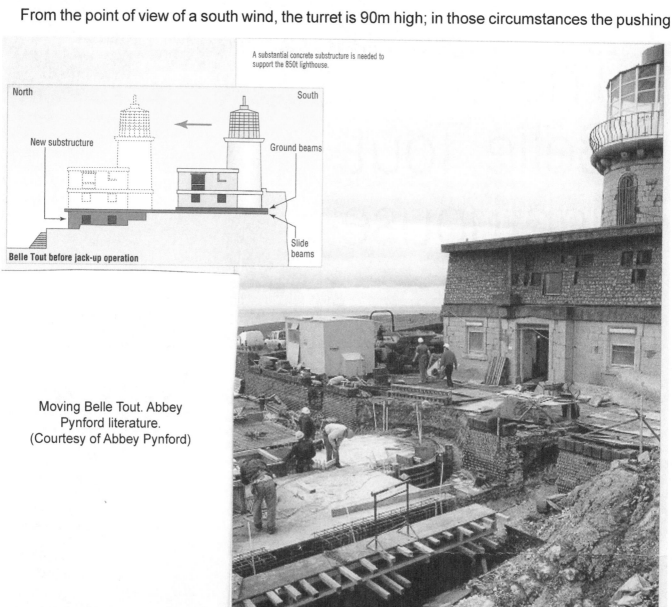

Moving Belle Tout. Abbey
Pynford literature.
(Courtesy of Abbey Pynford)

Moving Belle Tout.
(Picture courtesy of Chas Bell.)

jacks would be acting as brakes rather than rams. Six jacks were due to be deployed, acting between the grillage beams and temporary steel channels bolted onto the slide beams. This way, the jacking forces are transmitted to the ground under the length of the slide beams and through the foundations of the new structure, which are a lot further from the cliff edge.

Immediately before the slide began the whole structure had to be jacked back up off the cheeses and the grease skate assemblies inserted; 12 under the tower and 10 under the annexe. Inverted jacks link the skates to the structure, connecting together in three groups to form a three-legged, self-levelling hydraulic suspension system during the move. With the pushing jacks having a stroke of around 1,100mm, Abbey Pynford was planning for the final slide to take 17 jack cycles, each lasting around 30 minutes. Two days before that, however, a trial slide was scheduled.

An elaborate system of guides and laser monitors was to keep the structure on track during its main move. The final stages were the transfer of load to the 22 re-inserted jacks, the removal of the grease skates and the lowering of the structure onto a sand/cement bed on top of the new ground floor. A discrete application of mould oil should ensure that, when and if jacks are re-inserted preparatory to a second move sometime in the future, they should have no difficulty in separating the sections.

In spite of all the precautions a bomb scare at 11.28am halted the move for a few brief minutes. A concerned member of the public came across a shell and, being aware of the activity on the site, reported it to the organisers. This sparked a rumour that a bomb had been planted. Onlookers, press, public and engineers were all asked to leave, but five minutes later everyone was allowed back. It wasn't a bomb.

A few minutes into the move, proceedings came to a halt again, as chalk had started to fall away from the cliff. After rigorous checks that proved all was safe, movement began again at lunchtime. A spokesperson for Abbey Pynford said, 'We have only to rupture some of the structure and that would be the end of it.'

A-level students from Eastbourne College, acting as stewards, enjoyed a field trip to watch the move. Wayne Trinder, school's head of design and technology, hoped that witnessing the impressive operation would inspire Eastbourne's engineers of the future. 'We have a number of students who are going to do engineering at university. This shows them what it is really like out there for engineers.'

It was hoped to accomplish the move in one day, but with minor hold-ups and the repositioning of the jacks the lighthouse was only part of the way to its new home by the first evening.

Moving Belle Tout.
(Picture courtesy of Chas Bell)

At the end of the second day, as Belle Tout finally arrived and settled into her new resting place, a triumphant shower of fireworks lit up the night sky and lights in the lantern room pulsed out the message that the move was complete.

One of the coastguards present during the move was John Dann, whose father, Cecil, had worked at the lighthouse. He recalled that some 30 years ago he had worked for Mrs Cullinan when she lived there. 'I did the doors on the garages and sheds at the sides. I was surprised to see they were still there. My father also worked here as a handyman.'

By April a worrying internal crack had appeared in the living quarters. Mark Roberts commented that, 'the building has obviously flexed a little when we moved it ... It is really just a cosmetic plaster crack. We are not worried about it and the structure of the building is perfectly secure. It will now be made watertight and sealed into place.'

A tragedy occurred during the move when Alan Morrison, 43, from Nottingham, a television security guard working for the BBC outside broadcast team and guarding satellite dishes, was found dead by the camera crew in his camper van on 17 March. He is thought to have finished his shift and gone to his van to sleep. A gas ring was found to be switched on, and his death had been caused by carbon monoxide poisoning. At Eastbourne Magistrates Court, in September 1999, BW Security Ltd, his employer, and directors Graham White and Michael Burrows each admitted two health and safety issues. The company, from Lambley, Nottinghamshire, was fined £5,000 with £4,756 costs. White and Burrows were each fined £2,500. The van in question contained a defective gas blow heater, and the court heard that they had failed to carry out necessary safety checks.

LOUISE ROBERTS - DIARY FOR THE *EASTBOURNE GAZETTE*

Thursday, 11 March

Mark's birthday but he does not have much time to open his presents. We are frantically sending out invites for the move and producing timed tickets for all the people who bought a brick. I managed to get away briefly to register our baby, Quinn, who will be six weeks old tomorrow, and must be formally registered by then. The registrar asks how everything is going and wishes us well for Wednesday's move. It is amazing how much positive support local people have shown for this project.

Friday, 14 March – Mothers' Day

Mark is ill in bed with the flu. This is very bad timing but it is probably due to the build up of stress over the last few weeks. Belle Tout has been lifted 60cm to prepare for the final stages of beam work to be completed.

Monday, 15 March

Our family have come down to help with the final preparations and there is still much to do. We have a coach organised to take people from Beachy Head to Belle Tout, but today the driver announced he would not be able to turn around in the lay-by at the foot of Belle Tout and would need to go to Birling Gap. Disaster! We are worried he will not be able to keep our ticket timing.

Tuesday, 16 March

It is my 30th birthday, but with less than 24 hours to go there is no time to celebrate. Birthdays happen every year, you only move a lighthouse once in a lifetime. We finally got to bed around 2am, so much for an early night.

Wednesday, 17 March – day of the move

It is said that everyone is famous for a day. This is certainly our day. From 6am we were at Belle Tout and already the media were assembling ... Meridian, GMTV, BBC, ITN, French TV, German TV, and Japanese TV. Luckily we have Tim Cobb and Associates handling all the media and organising times for interviews. My sister was looking after baby Quinn, and although he needed feeding, I could not get away until 10am. By that time my throat was so dry I could hardly speak. The sun shone all day long as Belle Tout crept along to her new location. We had hoped she would be there by 7.30pm when *Tomorrow's World* did their live broadcast, but a few earlier technical problems had slowed things down, so there was still a third to go. However, whether it was exhaustion or relief Mark slept better tonight than he has done for many months.

Thursday, 18 March

Still feeling the euphoria from yesterday's events, we watched Belle Tout reach her final position. Over the past two years we have explained hundreds of times how the engineers planned to move Belle Tout. Seeing it for real and finally realising it is over was quite overwhelming.

Friday, 19 March

Inside for the first time! We need a 20ft ladder to reach our kitchen door now though! The magnificent views we had before are now even better. All our glass bottles are still perfectly in place.

Saturday, 20 March.

Our first weekend off for three months...

The Mail on Sunday, March 21, 1999

'It's not my fault. Somebody must have moved the lighthouse.'

Cartoon from "The Mail on Sunday."
(By kind permission of The Mail on Sunday.)

Right: Starting on 17 March 1999, the tower and living quarters were moved back 17m (50ft) on greased runners for another 25 years of life, at a cost of £15,000 per metre. Glass flower vases and other delicate items were quite safe on shelves all through the move.

51

The move. Origins of picture unknown

CHANGING ROOMS

Changing face of Belle Tout

THE SPOTLIGHT will be on Belle Tout Lighthouse again this week — but this time the whole nation is invited inside.

That's because the lighthouse — along with owners Mark and Louise Roberts — is to be featured on top TV design programme Changing Rooms.

The famous building became home to chief executive Sari Conway and husband Vince when the two couples swapped homes for three days.

On Tuesday on BBC1 at 8.30pm, viewers will be able to find out what happened when Sari and Vince were given the task to totally re-vamp the lantern of Belle Tout with a professional designer and, of course, Handy Andy.

Residents will also be able to see how Mark and Louise coped with giving Sari and Vince's bedroom in their Eastbourne home a breath of fresh air.

Programme host Carol Smillie basked in the Eastbourne sunshine when she visited in June to film the show.

Carol, who was heavily pregnant at the time, said she loved her three-day trip to the town.

'Eastbourne really is lovely,' she said, 'Normally, we film Changing Rooms in very built-up areas — so it was brilliant to be so close to such a fabulous coastline.'

She added, 'I've had a brilliant time and it was definitely one of the most enjoyable Changing Rooms I've presented.'

Mark Roberts said that both he and Louise had a great time filming the show.

'The weather was really good throughout, but we were worked very hard so there wasn't much time to enjoy it.

'It's always good to get Eastbourne on the television and show people all over the country that it's a great place to come on holiday.'

TOP: Louise and Mark Roberts meet Carol Smillie. *(Jun 228/9a)*

Mark and Louise Roberts – "Changing Rooms."
(Picture courtesy of T.R. Beckett Newspapers.)

Life went on. In June 1999 the Roberts' and Belle Tout were featured on a TV programme, *Changing Rooms*. They swapped homes with Eastbourne's Chief Executive Sari Conway and her husband Vince. Viewers were welcomed by programme host Carol Smillie, who said that she really loved her three-day trip to Eastbourne, 'Normally we film *Changing Rooms* in very built-up areas, so it was brilliant to be so close to such a fabulous coastline. It was definitely one of the most enjoyable programmes I've presented.'

Sari decorated Belle Tout's lantern room with the help of TV's 'Handy Andy'. The compass sketched on the ceiling was obliterated by blue paint, the knee-high wooden panels were given an antique look by mixing boot polish with brown paint, and the seating was refurbished. Drapes made from white shower curtains were hung around the glass panels.

The Roberts' revamped the bedroom in Sari's home, although things did not go that smoothly – as Mark Roberts had wanted to knock out a window and part of an exterior wall to put in patio doors. He even tried to book a double glazing company to do the job, but was told that this would use up much of the programme's limiting budget. The resultant write-up in the *Eastbourne Herald* stated, 'Carol Smillie was shocked; Handy Andy was gobsmacked and the producer was furious. Eventually Mark's grand plans hit the skids. However, the nautical theme of the lighthouse and Sari's chocolate-box bedroom were both a great success.'

QUESTIONS OF FINANCE

In July 1999 a political storm broke out because Eastbourne taxpayers were forced to fork out £7,000 for crowd control during Belle Tout's move. Mr Roberts, a Conservative councillor, told the local press that 'The road blocks were unnecessary; the Lib Dem-controlled council only decided the crowd control measures were necessary at the last minute. I think this was only initiated by the Lib Dems a couple of weeks after I said that I might be running for election. Initially, they were trying to get me to pay for the whole lot.'

At a meeting of the Eastbourne Environment Committee, spokesperson Bob Kirtley said, 'Expenditure of that size was not budgeted. I was one of the people on the Policy and Resources Committee who said under no circumstances should the people of Eastbourne bear the cost at all. I believe it generated publicity for Beachy Head instead of Eastbourne.'

Mr Roberts, defending the expenditure, replied, 'There were more than 140 media people there on the day. That's a record for Sussex. If Eastbourne did not benefit from that, you've got to ask how they allowed that to happen.'

THE HOLIDAY PROGRAMME

In October 1999 Belle Tout got another TV airing, this time on BBC1's *The Holiday Programme*. Presenter Craig Doyle and the film crew spent several nights at the lighthouse while filming an item on the Sussex downland. He said, 'The next time the eclipse comes around this lighthouse will either be in the water or 20m down the hill.' Louise Roberts said that she was delighted *The Holiday Programme* was using the lighthouse at its base for the four day visit. She added, 'This is a unique building in a unique part of Britain. *The Holiday Programme* has a reputation for producing informative and lively reports on destinations around the world, and I am sure that our beautiful Sussex downland will provide them with plenty of footage.'

Don Granger, USA visitor to Belle Tout in 1999.
(Picture courtesy of the Grangers and Michael Compton.)

HOLIDAY VISITORS TO BELLE TOUT

Janet Rokus and Jane Granger, USA visitors to Belle Tout in 1999.
(Picture courtesy of the Grangers and Michael Compton.)

Once Belle Tout was settled into its new site, the Roberts family again opened it up for bed and breakfast, charging £25 per head during the week and £35 at weekends. In September 1999 Jane and Don Granger and friend Janet Rokus came from Manteno, USA, to Eastbourne.

Jane said:
'My first knowledge of Belle Tout came about after meeting an Eastbourne resident Mick Compton in 1997 while he was on assignment to a pharmaceutical company in the US. He was assigned to the same department that I worked in, and I was asked to help get Mick acclimatised to the company and the surrounding area in Kankakee, Illinois. Mick soon became a good friend to me, my husband Don and friend Janet.

In 1999 he invited the three of us to his son's wedding. This was to be our first visit to Europe and we were very excited to be going. We arrived in late August of 1999 and visited many of England's famous areas. We never felt like tourists because Mick personally took us around many places of interest in England. The most interesting was staying in the Belle Tout lighthouse on Beachy Head. How many people can say they slept in a famous lighthouse? We were told by the lighthouse owners that we were the first Americans to stay there. The view of Beachy Head and the English Channel from the top of Belle Tout was breathtaking. Everything was so peaceful and relaxing. They had a Beagle dog called Nessie that was so friendly. I wish we could have stayed there longer than one night, but we were due to take the Eurostar to Brussels the next morning.'

They enjoyed the novelty and luxury of bathing in the raised cast-iron bath 'before departing from Belle Tout at 3.30am on a cool early September morning. We were to meet Mick at the bottom of the road leading from Belle Tout at 5.00am to catch the train. It was a beautiful early morning with the moon and stars shining brightly. I couldn't help feeling what I imagined the Von Trapp family fleeing the Germans in the dark may have felt like. I often think of our visit to Beachy Head and Belle Tout. We would rate our stay there as a 10.'

Mick Compton and wife Sue said:
'A friend of ours, Ken White, used to do odd jobs for the Foulkes family. He had a key and in September 1989 he asked us if we would like to go along with him one evening and have a look around Belle Tout, which has such an unusual layout. We sat in the lantern room and watched the sun set, we were just in awe of the view, and we've never lost the feeling for this building. Our little daughter, Helen, loved the lighthouse and we couldn't get her away from the lily pond. We've still got pictures of her sitting on the little wall surrounding it. She also loved the idea of the pull-down bunk bed in one of the tower rooms.

In the lantern room we were fascinated to find hundreds of sea shells decoratively embedded into the concrete. Outside, Paul Foulkes had cut a rough seat into the chalk at the top of the cliffs and he used to sit there, legs dangling over the edge, gazing out to sea.

We felt that this would be an ideal place for our American friends to stay, so when they visited in 1999, we went up there and made a booking for the 3rd September. As they didn't do evening meals at Belle Tout, we all went to the Beachy Head pub for dinner.

There is no doubt that Belle Tout has an aura, it draws you to the building, and there is a feeling of peace that enfolds you. It is nice to know that this little lighthouse is not going to be abandoned or neglected.'

In November 2011 sisters Naoko Yoshida and Sawako Gomi visited their friend Jill Rutherford in Eastbourne.

'As our visit was very short, we could only stay in Eastbourne for two days – therefore we wanted somewhere special to stay overnight, somewhere fascinating to us Japanese. Jill, who had written a book about Japan, in which we are mentioned, recommended the Belle Tout lighthouse and when we checked it out on the Internet, we just had to stay there. We were not disappointed. The breakfast was excellent and our rooms were exciting, interesting and very comfortable, the staff extremely friendly and helpful. And, of course, the views! They were stunning. We were fortunate in having perfect weather for November and the sun shone down on us. Belle Tout was a special and exciting place to stay and it will remain in our memories forever. We look forward to a return visit.'

Japanese visitors Naoko Yashida (left) with her sister Sawako Gomi (right)
With friend Jill Rutherford centre.
(Picture courtesy of Jill Rutherford.)

Reservation for at Belle Toute Lighthouse

26 August 1999

We look forward to welcoming you to Belle Toute Lighthouse and confirm your details as follows:

Date Booked   Room type   Price/ person / night Bed & Breakfast

03 September 1999   1 Double   35.00

Notes extra person on Z Bed £15

Finally, if there is anything else we can do to make your stay more enjoyable please call us on 01323 423 520.

Mark & Louise Roberts
Belle Toute Lighthouse

Confirmation Remittance
For
Mr M Compton

I wish to confirm my booking at Belle Toute Lighthouse for 1 Double from 3pm on Fri

Staying the nights of   03 September 1999

Please find enclosed a cheque made payable to Belle Toute Lighthouse for £_____

this being a 50% deposit against my booking

My phone number is 01323 502124

Our special request is _____

Signed_____   . Dated: 26 August 1999

Please send remittance to: Belle Toute Lighthouse, Beachy Head, East Sussex BN20 0AE
Receipt will only be issued if requested

Copy of Accommodation booking at Belle Tout, 1999.
(Courtesy of Michael Compton.)

Belle Toute Lighthouse
Beachy Head East Sussex BN20 0AE

Mr M Compton
▇▇▇▇▇▇▇▇▇▇
EASTBOURNE
BN22 9JB

26 August 1999

Dear Mr. Compton

Thank you for your booking and please find enclosed our brochure.

Our lighthouse sits high up on the beautiful white cliffs of Beachy Head, surrounded by open rolling downland and enjoying dramatic views across the ever changing sea. You will feel as if you are in perfect isolation and yet Eastbourne is only 10 minutes by car and Brighton 30 minutes.

You will be part of history by staying in the only occupied lighthouse in England. Our rooms all have double beds and whilst they enjoy lovely uninterrupted views you are welcome to enjoy the views throughout the lighthouse during your stay.

Close by we have an unspoilt traditional English pub, The Tiger, with open fires a village green, real ales and lovely home-made food. This, and indeed two further pubs, are a few minutes drive and also make a refreshing walk. For special occasions, we boast The 'Hungry Monk' at Jevington, a Michelin recommended restaurant and birthplace of Banoffi Pie! (bookings advisable 01323 482 178)

If you enjoy the rugged outdoors or just feel like a stroll along the beach, all is within easy reach. The 'Seven Sisters' makes an energetic walk and have you ever tried 'Tri-sailing' -kite powered go-karts - speeding along the cliff edge. Or take a boat along the coast and view Belle Toute from the sea.

Arrive before sunset and enjoy a quiet drink in the lantern over looking the sea and gently slip away from your regular routine. We look forward to welcoming you to our unique home and if you require any further information please phone 01323 423 520.

Your room will be ready from 3pm onwards and we ask that you call us about a week before your stay so we can ensure the access gates are open when you arrive. To confirm your booking we would like a deposit totalling 50% of your stay within seven days, (see attached remittance slip) with cheques made payable to 'Belle Toute Lighthouse' sent to the above address. On receipt of this your room will be guaranteed.

Yours sincerely,

Mark & Louise Roberts
Belle Toute Lighthouse

Copy of booking letter.
(Courtesy of Michael Compton.)

A Walk to the Beach

I walk the dusty green
Downland
Past Hawthorn bent and
bowed,
tired by the strong winters
breath
Still wild and freshening
on my face.

Distant cliffs, buttered by
a low sun,
standing firm and defensive
against the sea.
Both remain old
adversaries,
in a never ending battle.

Dropping down to the
beach now
Where the cold tentacles of
salt and froth
hold back,
I find such gentle curves of
chalk
and flint,
and more..

~Spend a night
in the only lighthouse,
in occupation,
in England~

The wild romantic setting
high up on 300ft cliffs
affords unique views and
breathtaking sunsets across
the Seven Sisters and
Beachy Head

~Take a refreshing walk to
one of the three nearby
pubs~

~Search for shipwreck
remains at Birling Gap
Beach~

Or wind your way up
the narrow stone stairs to
the top of the Lighthouse
and feel the beauty of
Beachy Head
whatever the weather

Belle Toute Lighthouse

Beachy Head
E Sussex
BN20 0AE

Phone
01323 423 520

www.btinternet.com · belle.tout

Brighton
35 min

Eastbourne
5 min

East Dean

A 259   Tiger
Inn

Birling Gap
Pub

Beachy
Head
Pub

Seven Sisters

Belle Tout Lighthouse

Copy of brochure for Belle Tout 1999.
(Courtesy of Michael Compton.)

The Life of Belle Toute Lighthouse

In the 1700's 'Parson Derby' concerned at the number of ships lost to the cliffs, dug a cave below Belle Toute hill, in the base of the cliff where he stood with a bright lantern to warn mariners of the danger approaching.

Subsequently, in the early 1800's a local character 'Mad Jack Fuller' constructed a wooden lighthouse at the cliff top which was so successful the decision was made to build Belle Toute as a permanent lighthouse in 1832.

Due to continuous cliff erosion and sea mists the effectiveness of Belle Toute waned and she was decommissioned in 1902, when the current red and white lighthouse took over.

Bed & Breakfast
Accommodation
£25 per person Sun to Thur.
£35 per person Fri & Sat
(double room)

Our three rooms
are
non smoking,
and have
private facilities.

Breakfast
Served from 8am
fresh fruit juice
~
tea, coffee, hot chocolate
~
toast
~
selection of fresh fruit
cereals
hot downland porridge
~
pork & leek sausages
smoked bacon, eggs
grilled tomato
mushrooms
or
daily specials such as,
scrambled eggs with smoked salmon
& dill
kippers
pancakes with maple syrup

The Life of Belle Toute Lighthouse

Over the following years Belle Toute was privately owned until after the Second World War when she sustained severe damage from friendly fire and the freehold was given to Eastbourne Council.

Happily Belle Tout was restored and we are now the first family to have the lighthouse as our permanent home.

We moved Belle Toute away from the cliff edge on the 17th of March 1999 which will prolong her lifetime by about 60 years, proceeds from your stay will go to assist with the project.

Menu at Belle Tout 1999.
(Courtesy of Michael Compton.)

GOOD MORNING

- MILK & OJ IS IN THE FRIDGE

- JUST CLICK BUTTON ON COFFEE MAKER
  FOR FRESH COFFEE

- THERE IS A BOWL OF FRESH FRUIT IN
  THE FRIDGE

- USE THE CORDLESS PHONE ON
  THE TABLE
        TYPE IN NO THEN PRESS GREEN
        BUTTON
        PRESS GREEN BUTTON TO HANG UP

- HELP YOURSELF TO TOAST IF YOU WISH !

- DO TAKE THE CARDS & BROCHURES WITH YOU.

      ENJOY THE REST OF YOUR HOLIDAY !

          LOUISE & MARK
          Belle Tout Lighthouse.

ANY PROBLEMS KNOCK ON OUR DOOR
(STRAIGHT AHEAD AT THE FOOT OF
THE BOTTOM STAIRS)

Note left by the Roberts for the Grangers.
(Courtesy of the Grangers and Michael Compton.)

SALE OF THE FREEHOLD

Although it was widely believed that there was a legal obligation by the council to keep Belle Tout lighthouse and the Eastbourne Downland in perpetuity for the people of the town, in February 2001 the Tory-run borough council said it would accept a sum of £900 from Mrs Louise Roberts for the purchase of the freehold. The council stated that it had been aware some two years earlier that it would be forced to sell. The Roberts' solicitor, Stephen Rimmer, of Stephen Rimmer and Co, Solicitors, wrote to the council in November 1998 asking that the freehold sale should go ahead. Under the terms of the 1967 Leasehold Reform Act, holders of long-term leases can buy out the freehold on their property when they have lived continuously at the accommodation for two years or more.

In a statement Mr Rimmer said, 'I asked the council to confirm the price payable would be calculated on the basis of the building in its cliff edge location. I believe that this is agreed as otherwise my client would, in effect, be penalised for moving the building.'

Shocked councillors said that they had been kept in the dark until the last minute until the arrangement was announced in a memo to members of the Downland Advisory Group. A spokesperson for Eastbourne Borough Council told the press: 'We do not normally discuss our property transactions but we have no control over the freehold which we were legally obliged to sell to Mrs. Roberts.'

Councillor Maurice Skilton, Chair of the Council's Strategic Planning and Corporate Resources Scrutiny Committee was quoted in the press: 'I think the sale of the freehold is a very sad step and I will do anything in my power to stop it. The whole thing is absolutely scandalous and I am going to call it in to my next Scrutiny Committee to get some complete answers.'

Councillor Beryl Healey, Lib Dem opposition leader, opposed the sale of Belle Tout's lease. She said, 'The downland belonged to the people of Eastbourne. The matter of the sale was kept very quiet.' She wanted the sale to be referred to the town's watchdog committee. But Ann Murray, Upperton ward Tory councillor, commented, 'It's a shame that it is passing into private hands, but the Act says if you are a leaseholder, you can buy after a certain time.'

Eastbourne's Lib Dems tried to prevent the sale of the lighthouse, but after a letter was sent to them by Stephen Rimmer, Lib Dem candidate Chris Berry said, 'I accept that Mrs. Roberts and the borough council have acted totally legally and done nothing wrong.'

The facts were as follows: the borough council, as landlords, had no right to block the sale in principle; Mrs Roberts had the legal right to purchase the freehold, having owned the leasehold for three years; and the district valuer advised the price to be set at £900 because it was a long lease. At the time of the agreement the lighthouse was in danger of falling into the sea, so the value was low.

Council leader Graham Marsden commented, 'In 1998 the Lib Dems knew that the valuation of the lease was less than £1,000, and the owners could purchase the freehold.'

On completion of the deal Councillor Roberts and Mrs Roberts would be able to do as they wished with Belle Tout, but Louise Roberts said, 'I have no plans to sell the lighthouse. This is our family home and we want it to stay that way. It was always our intention to purchase the freehold; this is the best way to preserve the building.'

Beryl Healey wanted the sale referred to the council's watchdog committee: 'Selling this high-profile site is of interest and importance to the people of Eastbourne and the decision-making process should be totally transparent. The Eastbourne Downland belongs to the people of Eastbourne. The matter was deliberately dealt with by an officer to keep it secret, instead of making it public. It should have been discussed at an open council meeting. This is about the council; it has been sneaky.'

Transfer of whole
of registered title(s)

HM Land Registry **TR1**

1. Stamp Duty

I/We hereby certify that this instrument falls within category ___ in the Schedule to the Stamp Duty (Exempt Instruments) Regulations 1987

[X] It is certified that the transaction effected does not form part of a larger transaction or of a series of transactions in respect of which the amount or value or the aggregate amount or value of the consideration exceeds the sum of

£ 60,000

2. Title Number(s) of the Property
EB11828

3. Property

BELLE TOUT LIGHTHOUSE, EASTBOURNE, EAST SUSSEX

4. Date
6ᵗʰ March 2001

5. Transferor

THE COUNCIL OF THE BOROUGH OF EASTBOURNE

6. Transferee for entry on the register

LOUISE ANITA ROBERTS

7. Transferee's intended address(es) for service in the U.K. *(including postcode)* for entry on the register

Belle Tout Lighthouse, Beachy Head, Eastbourne, East Sussex. BN20 0AB

8. The Transferor transfers the property to the Transferee.

9. Consideration

[X] The Transferor has received from the Transferee for the property the sum of
NINE HUNDRED POUNDS (£900)

___ The Transfer is not for money or anything which has a monetary value

Copy of transfer of the whole of the registered title of Belle Tout o Louise Roberts.
(Courtesy of David Shaw.)

THE FINANCIAL SCANDAL

On 16 May 2001 the *Eastbourne Herald* ran a front page headline: 'Belle Tout Charity Never Existed – Councillor admits lighthouse cash not accounted for', and an article by reporter Adam McNaught-Davis stated:

Tory councillor Mark Roberts admitted financial irregularities at Belle Tout lighthouse. The *Herald* can today reveal a registered charity set up to house public donations for the lighthouse move never existed. And thousands of pounds worth of donations has not been accounted for. Accounts were never prepared. The holding account for up to £20,000 of public money was a limited liability company, The Southdown Lighthouse Trust Ltd.

This has now been struck off by Companies House after failing to produce accounts during nearly three years of trading. Despite these facts, Cllr Roberts, who lives at the landmark property with his wife Louise – the owner of the building – gave the impression in headed letters that donations were destined for regulated charity coffers.

Several pieces of letter-headed material state 'a charity' and give a registration number. The Charities Commission ordered Cllr Roberts to change the wording when it was alerted earlier this year.

A commission spokesperson said, 'Following concerns about the Southdown Lighthouse Trust, the Charity Commission wrote to the organisation and told it to remove the claim that it was a registered charity. By this time the business was dissolved.

The commission confirmed an application for charity status had been received in February 1998, but it was withdrawn following commission advice.

Mark Roberts replied to the accusations:

We initially set up the Southdowns Lighthouse Trust and made an application to the Charity Commission because only registered charities can receive funds from the Heritage Lottery to which we were applying for a grant. Unfortunately, we did not obtain this charity registration and should have made people aware of this. We sincerely and genuinely apologise for any confusion this has caused.

Also we should have prepared the Southdowns Lighthouse Trust accounts and apologise for not actioneering this sooner. Accounts will be with Companies House by the end of this month, we had instructed this to be done before being contacted by the *Eastbourne Herald*.

Following huge public interest in the saving of Belle Tout, we began a 'Buy a Brick' fundraising campaign. People paid £10 to 'buy a brick' and the money was collected by Eastbourne Borough Council through the Tourist Information Centre. In return for this money, people received a certificate of thanks and an invitation to the once-a-lifetime moving day.

There will also be a commemorative plaque erected once the final engineering work is completed. A handling fee of 10 per cent was also charged by the Tourist Information Centre.

We are very appreciative of all monies donated and in the end it was only local people who did contribute as no major funding (e.g. Lottery) was forthcoming.

We raised approximately £5,000 from the 'Buy a Brick' which went towards the total cost of £250,000.

The remaining £245,000 was paid by ourselves, personally. We did not receive any money from Eastbourne Borough Council.

On Friday 1 June 2001 the *Eastbourne Herald* reported that Mark Roberts had offered a 'full refund' to all the 341 'Buy a Brick' donors. In a letter he stated, 'If you have read or heard anything which still leaves you feeling unsure of what happened to your money and are unhappy to support the project we will be happy to refund in full any 'Buy a Brick' monies ... We ultimately personally funded the majority of the move, which cost £250,000 with approximately £5,000 raised through 'Buy a Brick.' Other funds collected through bed and breakfast and open days took the total amount raised to approximately £9,000. Full accounts will be lodged.'

In late June 2001, prompted by complaints from several Eastbourne residents, an investigation was instigated by the Charity Commission regarding the claim by Councillor Mark Roberts that the South Downs Lighthouse Trust Ltd was a registered charity: 'Following further complaints we are now looking into the grounds on which the money was raised and the money's application. We are in correspondence with representatives of the Belle Tout Lighthouse and will be meeting with them soon.'

In reply, Mr Roberts said:

'There is a meeting scheduled with the Charity Commission to discuss the applications of the funds collected by the South Downs Lighthouse Trust. It is not a formal enquiry and we are looking forward to this opportunity to present the facts regarding the money raised to save Belle Tout and are confident of the outcome...

May I reiterate that the South Downs Lighthouse Trust had a total income of approximately £9,800 of which £5,000 was from Buy-a-Brick donations and the remainder from open days, proceeds from bed and breakfast and other minor events (not donations). The total project cost in the region of £250,000.

We have had many letters of support from people who bought a brick and wish to thank them for their kind words. We sincerely and genuinely apologise for any confusion this has caused. Also, we should have prepared the Southdown Lighthouse Trust accounts and apologise for not actioning this sooner. Accounts will be with Companies House by the end of this month.'

But a Companies House spokesperson said, 'If they submitted accounts now we would have nowhere to put them. The company is dissolved.'

But the accusations wouldn't go away. Barry Lane wrote in the *PIE* (People In Eastbourne) community magazine in 2001:

The Mark Roberts scandal deepens as it emerges that the accountant who helped 'clear' the councillor's name at the Charity Commission had been a co-director of the Belle Tout 'charity', but resigned when he discovered that Roberts was running it as a scam.

Accountant Ian Killick left his co-director's post in 1998 after learning that the Southdowns Lighthouse Trust (SLT) had been refused charity status by the Commission, but that Cllr Roberts was running it as if it were a legitimate good cause and was posing as a genuine trustee. Mr Killick also claims that he uncovered 'financial irregularities' ...

More extraordinary still, perhaps, the accountant – who unbelievably continues to represent Roberts on behalf of his employer, the accountancy firm Plummer Parsons – also claims that the Charity Commissioners were made aware that Roberts had run his company as an unregistered charity, but had 'acquitted' him anyway.

This bizarre twist brings into question the roles of Mr Killick, of Roberts' solicitor, Stephen Rimmer, who represented both Cllr and Mrs Roberts at the meeting with the Commissioners, and the Commission itself. The parts played by Roberts and his wife Louise – herself a former co-director of SLT – are already under the microscope.

In a typically misleading interview reported in the *Eastbourne Herald* on Friday 13th July, Roberts claimed that with the Charity Commission's report 'the truth' was at last emerging. On the contrary, it is quite clear that Cllr Roberts believes that the Commission has joined him in his futile bid to keep the truth well and truly concealed. *PIE*'s legal team has now written to the Charity Commission in an attempt to unravel this shameful case once and for all.

Roberts has again claimed that he is preparing to hand over the accounts of his so-called charity to Companies House even though they insist that a defunct company such as his cannot hand over accounts after it has been struck off for failing to provide them in the first place. A company should, of course, present its accounts at the appropriate time, when legally obliged to do so, not when it feels like belatedly cobbling together a few figures.

Many of the Australian-born councillor's difficulties are a result of his knack of persuading people to buy bricks for his home, Belle Tout lighthouse, when he moved it back to safety from the cliff edge near Beachy Head in March 1999. Donors convinced they were supporting a real charity paid up to £60 for a brick, but Roberts had failed ... to keeping records of the money he was given. A former employee even accuses him of pocketing cash donations.

According to the Commission's statement, Roberts had convinced them that he had written to as many of the people who had donated to his fake charity as he could recall, and apologised and returned the money. Of the duped donors *PIE* has traced so far, not one has received a single penny, although others may have been repaid without our knowledge.

One Meads resident, who bought five bricks at £10 each, is still awaiting his letter and the repayment which the Charity Commission is apparently convinced he must already have received. Cllr Roberts' fondness for paying bills with bouncing cheques should be enough to persuade donors to request cash or postal orders.

In a press statement the Charity Commission said it was satisfied that Roberts has operated SLT only in the 'anticipation' that it would have become a registered charity. It either failed utterly to dig sufficiently deep to learn that Roberts had continued to lie about the so-called Trust's status long after his application had been refused in 1998, or ignored the facts altogether.

A depressingly large number of business people have volunteered information about the town's least favourite Antipodean. As reported last month, Roberts has the worst attendance of any of Eastbourne's elected representatives, and to make matters worse he has managed to run up long-overdue debts with a staggering number of the town's business community – many of them in his own ward...

Roberts appears to rely upon people not being able to afford the time or the money to pursue him. For this reason, *PIE*'s own legal team is offering to bring a class action on behalf of businesses or individuals owed money by the councillor. He would find it a great deal more difficult avoiding a legal challenge of that size and clout...

In spite of generous offers from Eastbourne residents to support *PIE* financially should Roberts think he could sue us and get away with it, our doormat remains uncluttered by writs. This is unsurprising, for the weight of evidence against him is great, and growing, and only the Charity Commission and Sussex Police remain unconvinced.

Where will he turn next? The windfall from the sale of his interest in the pub will tide him over for a while and may even help to pay back one or two brick-buyers, but the £60 a week Eastbourne Borough Council pays him so generously for doing so little on its behalf is unlikely to get him far. He could, of course, try to persuade his wife to sell Belle Tout to raise a few hundred thousand pounds, but acquaintances believe that Mrs. Roberts may no longer be quite so well disposed towards her husband...

Meanwhile, back at the lighthouse, regular walkers and workers on the Downland near Belle Tout were amused to see that a public-spirited person had pinned a copy of last month's *PIE*, with its cover photo of Cllr Roberts, in a transparent bag on a notice-board adjacent to the entrance to Belle Tout. Some visitors were apparently seen photographing the magazine with Belle Tout as a backdrop to their pictures.

Other callers who stopped at Belle Tout were less amused. Two gentlemen in suits claimed they were bailiffs from London looking for Cllr Roberts. Happy locals eagerly pointed them in the direction of Cllr Roberts' UK Council Ltd office. One must hope they made it before their quarry's departure...

Roberts has countless questions to answer, of course, but so does Eastbourne Borough Council, who obligingly offered to help him collect donations for his fictitious charity in return for 10% of the take, even though they knew his reputation and were well aware by this time that his credit rating was rock bottom. Why did it fail to do its job on behalf of the people of Eastbourne and run a two-minute check to see if SLT was a genuine registered charity?

On the online Sussex History Forum, 'Pete' says, 'there were a lot of unanswered questions locally about how and why the funding to move it happened. I don't think there was ever a 'clean' answer.'

RENTING OUT BELLE TOUT, 2002

In March 2002 the Roberts' made the decision to rent Belle Tout for between £2,500 and £3,000 per calendar month. Advertising literature issued by the letting agents, Strutt and Parker, read as follows:

The property's heritage, location and stunning views make this lighthouse very attractive to the lettings market. It has five bedrooms, three of which are en-suite, an entrance hall, fitted kitchen, dining area, sitting area, utility room and a lantern room.

Situated three miles from the village of East Dean, Belle Tout lies in a wonderful location. The Horseshoe Plantation, famous for its rare migrating birds, and endangered British orchids, is nearby. Eastbourne town centre, which has a wide range of shopping facilities, schools, colleges, entertainment and main-line railway station, is just five miles away ... Belle Tout is one of the most unusual and historical lettings we shall be handling this year. Full particulars on the letting are available for a charge of £5.00.

BUILDING A NEW ACCESS ROAD

On 30 October 2002 an application was made for 'The Grant of an easement to resite access road':

Purpose: To consider and agree whether Eastbourne Borough Council should grant easement across the open Downland for the construction of a new access track to replace the existing track, which has become dangerous.

Recommendations: That delegated authority be given to the Director of Tourism and leisure in consultation with the Legal Section, to negotiate the granting of a new easement over Eastbourne Downland.

Background: In 2001, the leaseholder at Belle Tout served a 'Notice of tenants' claim to acquire the freehold or an extended lease for the property. Following this, the freehold of Belle Tout was transferred under the Leasehold Reform Act 1967 as required.
Part of the legal agreement was the continued easement rights over the Open Downland, owned by the Council, to allow the Freeholder access to Belle Tout over the existing track from the road.

Detail: The cliff edges along the Downland coastal fringes are continually eroding, which resulted in the moving of Belle Tout in 1999.
Unfortunately, the continued erosion in this area is now as close as one metre of the existing track and has become dangerous for the freeholder and members of the public who tend to use the track when viewing Belle Tout.
Signs have been placed to direct the public from the cliff edge, but access for post, refuse and utility services is no longer advisable.
In late 2002, the freeholder approached the Council regarding the need to move the access track for safety-in the short term and continued access provision to Belle Tout in the long term, for which a planning application would need to be submitted.

On 27 February 2003 a meeting was arranged for the freeholder to meet all interested parties which included English Nature, English Heritage, County Archaeologist, Sussex Downs Conservation Board, South Downs Way Officer, as well as Council Officers from Planning, Downland, Tree and Woodlands, Highways and Legal Services. The meeting proved useful in establishing a number of factors to guide the freeholder in completing a planning application.

Factors to consider included:
Route of proposed new access track.
Siting of junction with public highway.
Materials for access construction.
Effects of access track on grass and flora within the Site of Special Scientific Interest.
Effect of access track on ancient monument and archaeologically sensitive area.
The reinstatement of the existing access track.

On 11 June a planning application was received from the freeholder but there was insufficient information or detail in the application to allow any views on its suitability.

After discussing the matter in detail with the Head of Planning, a letter was sent giving more detail of those requirements and the consultations needed to progress the matter.

We have now received the site survey with entrance details and cross sections that were required, but are still, at this time, awaiting a detailed method statement on how materials and machinery will be stored. We will also need to know how the works will be carried out to minimise any peripheral damage to the Downland turf and flora during the excavation and construction process.

Consultations: This matter has been discussed with all parties ... and further discussion and consultations will take place leading up to and during the course of the works to ensure that any problems that may arise are minimised and resolved.

Financial
Implications: There are likely to be some costs for the legal sections time and liaison on site, but it should be agreed, prior to proceeding, that the freeholder will cover any legal and supervisory costs that the Council may incur.

Environmental
Implications: Great care will need to be taken over the detail in the method statement, to ensure that all parties are satisfied that only the minimum disruption of the area will be caused. This can be achieved by Officers maintaining close liaison on site, with the contractor, and regular communication with English Nature, English Heritage and County Archaeologist.

Human Resource
Implications: Time will need to be allocated to keep a watching brief during the site works, but it should be possible to accommodate this within our current resources.

Conclusion: If approved, it should be possible to minimise any extensive damage to the Open Downland. But this can only be achieved if all parties sign up to a carefully planned and implemented plan of operation and method statement.

Mike Smith
Downland Trees and Woodland Manager.

THE SALE OF BELLE TOUT

RAGER&ROBERTS

ESTATE AGENTS & VALUERS

36 Cornfield Road, Eastbourne. Telephone: 01323 430133

website: www.ragerroberts.co.uk   e-mail: sales@ragerroberts.co.uk

BELLE TOUTE LIGHTHOUSE

Belle Toute has unique location with breathtaking views over some of the finest coastal scenery in southern England. The accommodation comprises sitting room with dining area and kitchen, principal bedroom suite with dressing room and en suite shower room, 4 further bedrooms and lantern room.

Price Guide £595,000

Belle Tout up for sale in 2007.
(Courtesy of Rager and Roberts.)

Belle Tout –for sale. View of north side.
(Picture courtesy of Dowsett Associates.)

Belle Tout – for sale. View of west side.
(Picture courtesy of Dowsett Associates.)

By May 2007 the Roberts' had decided to sell their lighthouse and move to Australia. Strutt and Parker, the estate agents, said of the building, 'It is quite out of the ordinary. We can see it being sold as a second home or going to an artist or writer. It would still make a fantastic b & b, though it is probably not ideal for somebody with vertigo.'

The property description reads as follows:

Are you the new lighthouse family? Famous landmark, Belle Tout lighthouse which sits on the edge of the infamous Beachy Head in East Sussex, is for sale through national property specialists Strutt and Parker for a price guide of £850,000; this is an opportunity to purchase a famous and important landmark lighthouse with uninterrupted views over some of the most spectacular coastal scenery in southern England.

Internally, the lighthouse provides deceptively spacious, well proportioned and bright accommodation, principally over three floors. On the first floor there is a magnificent open plan living space which benefits from large picture windows that take full advantage of the magnificent views.

Other features include wood and stone floors, an open fireplace in the sitting room, a spacious principal suite with circular bedroom, high ceilings, a circular bathroom with central bath and a spiral staircase which leads up to the lantern room on the third floor, from which there are spectacular 360 degree views.

The lighthouse is approached over a long down land track that leads to a pair of wrought iron gates, opening onto a wide parking area to the south of the property, with two store rooms to one side.

Surrounding the lighthouse is a lawned garden enclosed by flint and brick walls. Immediately to the north of the lighthouse, curved steps lead down to an ornamental pond with water lilies. The remainder of the garden is laid to lawn with paved terraces and paths.

Sonia Purnell, writing for the *Daily Telegraph* in 2007, viewed the property: 'Now a surprisingly comfortable, if vertical, six bedroom, Grade II house, here is a property which, for once, really does command '360 degree views' ... It would not suit either keen gardeners or the immaculately coiffed, as the clifftop location combines with a rampant rabbit population to destroy all plant life ... a typical daily 'breeze' would rearrange even the starchiest hairdo ...'

Louise Roberts said, 'We have never bothered hanging pictures, there never seemed to be any point because the views would always be better.' The family stressed that they hoped Belle Tout would be bought by someone who would appreciate its 'differentness'. 'It's not ever going to be a smart minimalistic palace. It's for people who like living with nature.' She added, 'My son, Quinn, knows just how special this place is, and he has vowed, that whenever it is, and whatever it takes, one day Belle Tout will be his again.'

BELLE TOUT PRESERVATION TRUST

Businessman Rob Wassell had always been fascinated by Belle Tout:

'When I was a youngster we used to have family outings to Beachy Head. We'd walk from Birling Gap, over the top of the hill, and there was Belle Tout. I can remember going up to it, admiring it, and you could even get around the front of it then. When I passed my driving test and got a car, I used to often come this way, and you could see this building from all angles.

In 2007, on my way to Eastbourne, I stopped off at Belle Tout. It is very difficult to explain, there's a magic about it, and I was drawn to it. I spent a lot of time there that day, taking photographs, and when I went home and told my Dad that I'd been there, he said, 'You know it's for sale, don't you?' In my mind I thought it would be brilliant if I could buy it and open it up to the public. I had never done anything like this before, but I was driven, in my heart it felt right. I am an experienced project manager, so I logically planned everything out. I went to see Louise Roberts, who was selling it, and as I stepped in the door, it was like I was home. It was so familiar; I knew just where everything was.'

Eager to pursue his dream, Rob contacted the National Trust and English Heritage, both of whom had a vested interest in this unique building, to put them in the picture. He began to work through the project and had a valuation done; this was £650,000. 'It was my original intention that if 650,000 people each put in £1, it would be ours.'

Rob then set up the Belle Tout Lighthouse Preservation Trust. The trust's website, www.belletout. org.uk/trust.html, describes it as follows:

A not-for-profit organisation limited by guarantee with charitable objects and aims. It has been formed with the sole aim of purchasing and maintaining the Belle Tout lighthouse that is situated on the cliffs at Beachy Head, near Eastbourne, in the south of England ... The lighthouse ... is part of our national heritage and we firmly believe that it should be opened to the public and to maintain it for future generations of visitors to enjoy ... Trust ownership ensures that all of the profits from its business are re-invested back into the property to ensure that it is maintained and renovated. In addition to which, it will provide the money to pay for costs when the lighthouse requires moving again in the future. Local employment would greatly benefit with services that the lighthouse would need, such as builders, solicitors, architects, gardeners and staff to serve the guests and visitors.

The council's planning committee gave the go-ahead for the building to be opened to the public as long as the original access road, now perilously close to the cliff edge, was no longer used. Liberal Democrat Jon Harris commented that he was worried about public safety if people continued to use the old access road. He added, 'You hear about people using their sat nav and ending up on railway lines. What will we do if somebody goes up that road, their sat nav tells them to turn left and they end up over the cliff?' But fellow Lib Dem Michael Bloom replied, 'this is such a national symbol we should be promoting it as a tourist attraction and whatever we can do to encourage the applicant, we should.'

Rob Wassell told the media, 'We successfully received conditional planning permission to build the new access road. As this was already high on our list of plans this will be done anyway. We can now plough on to raise the money we need to buy the lighthouse. We hope the public's generosity will ensure the public themselves get the opportunity to visit the lighthouse and spend time there to learn of its history, how it was moved, what our plans are, whilst at the same time admiring the view and sipping tea.'

Everything went brilliantly at first: legal documents were in place and donations were being

Rob Wassell – Belle Tout Preservation Trust. Pictured at the lighthouse
(Picture courtesy of Rob Wassell.)

taken on line. 'Our biggest break came when the BBC said they wanted to cover all this live on the *One Show*.' A call centre was primed to take donations during the event: 'this was Friday night and the producer said he would like to have us on air the following Monday. They wanted to film at the lighthouse, with an outside broadcast crew.'

But shortly afterwards came the news that an offer had been received, and a disappointed Rob felt that it would be inappropriate to continue. 'I said, let's put it on hold for the moment, but if it comes back on the market again, we'll have another go. I was pretty devastated to be honest, after all these months and months of work, but I had a feeling we hadn't yet finished. So I phoned the estate agent and asked them to keep me in the picture.'

In early 2008 Belle Tout came back on the market at a lower price of £595,000.

'Wheels went back in motion, and I decided to get support from people with money who want to do something with it, and three people offered sums in excess of £100,000. Then the producer of the *One Show* got in touch and said that he wanted to feature all of this the following night. I was asked to get as many people as I could up to the lighthouse, and I thought, at last, this is it. To come back like this is incredible. Then the producer phoned to say that someone higher up than him had decided to go with another story. But he assured me that he would get me onto the show, but it didn't happen. Then I heard that Belle Tout had been sold to David Shaw. I thought, well, there's got to be a reason for this, whatever is meant to be. So I turned my attention to other projects.'

Rob eventually met David and Barbara Shaw:

'It was at Gatwick airport, which, initially, was nerve wracking, I didn't even know what they looked like, but as soon as they came through that door, I knew it was them. We sat down, and we had a really pleasant time. They were very passionate about what they wanted to do, and very excited about the project and I was very open about what I wanted. I took all the plans and we found out that our plans for the lighthouse were very similar. We got on brilliantly, it was heart-warming. We kept in touch.

Part of what I do through my company, RAW-systems, is website design. I already had my own personal Belle Tout website and when David said he needed one to promote the lighthouse B&B, I offered to do it as I had most of the information already. I am so honoured to still be involved with the lighthouse; it is a very special building.'

DAVID AND BARBARA SHAW

It is quite a jump from running a travel agency and delivering yachts built in the UK to becoming 'lighthouse keepers'. The new owners, who paid £500,000 for Belle Tout on 14 March 2008, are David and Barbara Shaw from Tenerife, who freely admitted they bought this unique building 'in a moment of madness with our hearts rather than our heads'.

They founded the Travel Shop in Tenerife in the 1980s, principally selling flights for journeys between the Canary Islands and the UK to ex-pats and Spanish. 'People were coming here and wanting to buy property, much of it being snapped up before it was built.' However, by the 1990s the good days were over. 'Nothing lasts for ever. We were in Tenerife when a friend phoned and told us that Belle Tout was for sale. We were very familiar with it because, in anticipation of our return to the UK, we had bought a house on the South Downs overlooking the sea, and in the middle of the view is this very lighthouse.'

The sale was slightly soured because a number of extra items, including a rather attractive stone lamp in the shape of a lighthouse, for which David had paid an additional £1,000, were not left by the Roberts' when they moved out. What they did leave, however, 'was a huge amount of rubbish which took many skips to clear!' The Roberts' oldest child, Haven, left a small present: a tin of fish food for the goldfish in the lily pool; with it was a note, 'Please look after my fish.' She would be pleased to know that some years later they are still there, and thriving.

The Shaws said, 'We would like to restore Belle back to its former glory because it is currently a little dilapidated and needs some work doing. We may have to move it further back from the cliff edge as we would like to give it a shelf life of 100 years rather than 20 or 30 years. But we have plans to turn it into a bed and breakfast business and a tea shop for walkers.'

Belle Tout was indeed shabby; much work was needed to bring it up to a high standard. David Shaw confessed that, having become the owner, he stood back and briefly thought, 'Oh my goodness, what have I done?'

Initially the Shaws had thought about living at the lighthouse themselves, but Barbara preferred to stay at their house. With David often away on business, she thought the location too isolated.

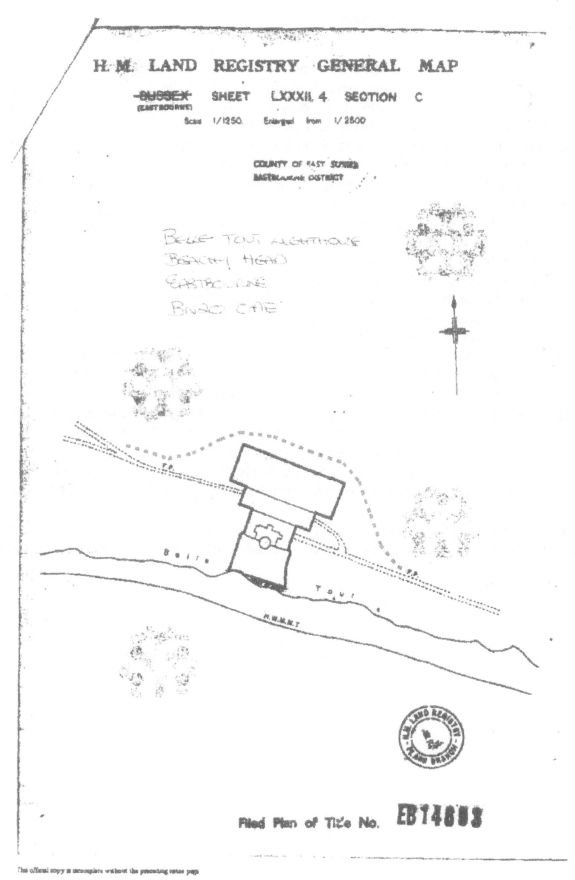

Land Registry Map of Belle Tout and adjacent land. Dated 13.02.08.

PLANNING ADVISORS AND ARCHITECTURAL CONSULTANTS

Tim Dowsett of Dowsett Associates, Hailsham, East Sussex, writes:

'We were approached by David Shaw in the early part of 2008 to assist him with planning issues that had arisen following his purchase of Belle Tout. This meant there were a lot of issues to be addressed from Day One. First we had to find out as much as we could about the legalities of the situation. We talked to the council as well, because we found out that there were a lot of enforcement notices that hadn't been served. But they were about ten years old and the Council were more interested in working with us. We wanted to know about the Grade II element of it, the Ancient Monument, and who we needed to talk to. We organised a series of 'round table' meetings with the Council to start with, to make quite sure everyone was on board and happy with what was going on. We talked to the Conservation Officer, the Highways Officer, because of the access element, the Downland authorities, because the new access road was going over the Downs, so they were involved in the types of materials used and the methodology and so on. There was also a condition on the planning permission relating to archaeology, so a county archaeologist needed to be involved with the site. We thought, this is going to be quite a job to do, principally because of what it was and where it was. We could see the new access road across the downland was going to be very sensitive. We could also see from the 2003 application and the conditions on it relating to the type of materials to be used and the methodology, the main thing is the Council wanted it to be done by hand. We knew that was going to be a difficult task.

Regarding the lighthouse, as with all listed buildings Noel Wells and I deal with, the first major complication was that it was a derelict building requiring building regulations and planning, and that is always a bit of a conflict. Fire and building regulations require you to do certain things as regards insulation and the windows and the way you deal with the fabric as well. We tried to bring the two together, which I think we did quite successfully in the end. The windows were already double-glazed, so we were replacing like with like. Inside, it was the fabric of the building, sanitary fittings, doors, all the sort of things you need to do to make it very nice bed and breakfast accommodation, compared with what was there.

It was our job to deal with the planning application for any changes, the Listed Building application for any changes, and the building regulation drawings. The Council were quite specific about what we needed to do to the building. The fire element of the building was difficult to achieve with the necessary fire escapes through the building, because when you are into several storeys it is a different ball game with fire protection.

Having completed all the applications, we presented them to the Council and eventually after conflicts and problems they were all approved. There were already previously agreed planning permissions for the B&B and the new road, so, to a certain extent the Council's hands were tied. But they realised whatever we did, it was going to be an improvement to the building.

Water coming into the lower level had been caused by the move and the floors were very spongy. We weren't contracted to do project supervision, our instructions and acceptance of us, was to deal with the planning, the Listed Building and the building regulations. We got all the permissions, and then the access road became an issue. I got involved with this, because I said to David Shaw, 'We've got a 2003 permission which expires in spring 2010. I said these days to get that again you would have to go through so many hoops; it wasn't even worth thinking about. So I said, 'You really must start that permission that you've got as we are just months away from its expiry date.'

The agent who had got the original planning permission for the new road was John Ball, of Building Design, in Eastbourne. He had undertaken numerous surveys and various drawings, which we could not replicate, so we needed him to come on board, because we needed to comply with the conditions of that 2003 permission before it expired. We actually managed to get mini-diggers on site just hours before those conditions ran out. We couldn't start on the downland section because we hadn't completed the negotiations with Eastbourne Borough Council. Where the access road came into Belle Tout, by starting that section, we had complied with the conditions and could carry on at any time. As John Ball had previously been involved with the exterior we said to him, 'You stay with the exterior; Noel and I will deal with the building, to avoid any conflict.'

The major issue to be settled was the construction of a new access road to Belle Tout and this was across downland owned by Eastbourne Borough Council and which Natural England had an interest in. The existing track was eroding due to the falling cliffs and in one area was very close to the cliff edge.

Planning permission had been granted for the access in 2004 and this had a five year life before it expired. There was also the question of unfinished negotiations with Eastbourne Borough Council for the easement and these proved difficult and protracted.

The Council wanted the new road, which is made of concrete blocks, to be sown with grass in between, so it would grow and cover the concrete. But this was impractical, as it would have made it very slippery when wet. There was also some element of the Ancient Monument, which is a mound in that area, which the archaeologist wanted to keep an eye on.

As regards Belle Tout itself, you really cannot appreciate how bad it was in its original state, it was pretty raw. What is now in place is unbelievable. It hasn't actually been added to, although when the building was moved, there was an extra ground floor added, to compensate for the sharp drop in the ground. I said, if they keep moving it, it will be like a block of flats.

Personally, I'm pleased with it. If someone said 'Were you involved with Belle Tout, I'd say that I was proud at what we have achieved. Perhaps we might not have done things quite the same way from day one, but I'm happy as to how it's turned out. It's nice to see it being used.

When you think what David Shaw has spent on that building, bearing in mind how close to the cliff edge it is, you've got to be honest to realise what's going to happen to it at some stage. Therefore it is fitting that this is a tribute to the building when it goes, that a lot of people will be using the building, enjoying it, enjoying the views, it is giving a lot of people a lot of pleasure.

The fact that many of the conditions attached to the planning application had not been complied with probably assisted, in a perverse sort of way, as David Shaw was able to put his views forward and in order to rectify the situation at Belle Tout they were largely accepted, and we were able to provide sketch plans for replacement windows and in some cases replacing windows or doors which had been blocked up. In particular, there was one door on the first floor (originally the ground floor prior to the move) which appeared rather incongruous at that level.

In addition to planning issues there was an urgent need to comply with Building Regulations as much of the building did not comply with basic requirements.

The first issues that were discussed related to the future use of Belle Tout which had the benefit of a 2007 planning application for a change of use to bed and breakfast accommodation, and in fact, the previous owners had operated such a business from Belle Tout after the move. Consideration was given to using the building as part residential and part bed and breakfast use and also possibly incorporating a walkers tea rooms. However, it was eventually agreed to go with the 2007 permission to convert the property to bed and breakfast accommodation (with a manager's residential unit) and work started in this respect.

Throughout the process it had to be remembered that Belle Tout was a Listed Building and part of the external area was scheduled as an Ancient Monument and planning, listed building consent and building regulations had to be prepared accordingly. This meant there had to be constant dialogue with the planners and more particularly the Conservation Officer. Incidentally, the occupant of this post changed several times during the process, to add to the complications.

David Shaw also considered from the start of his ownership the possibility of a further move of

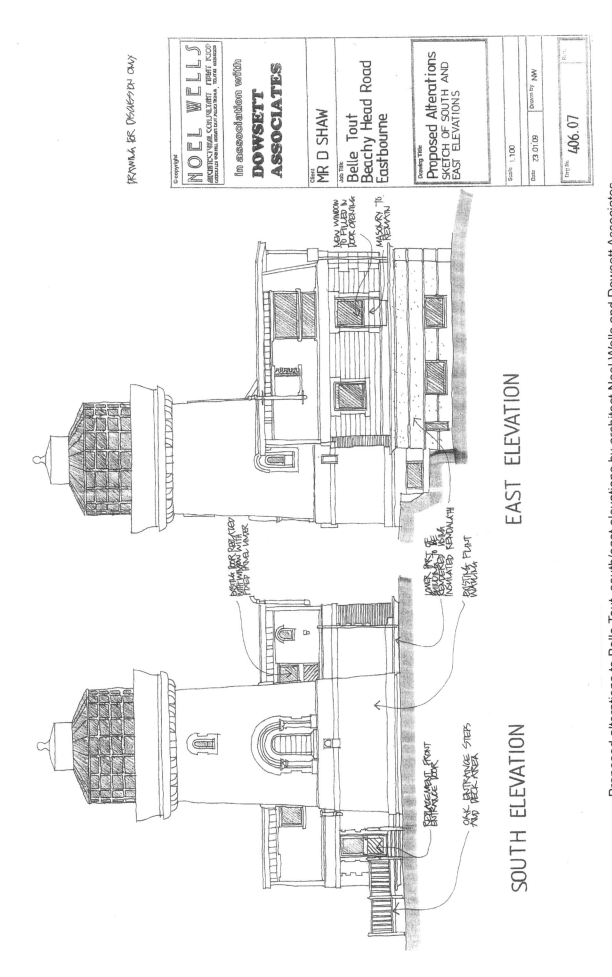

Proposed alterations to Belle Tout, south/east elevations by architect Noel Wells and Dowsett Associates
(Courtesy of Dowsett Associates)

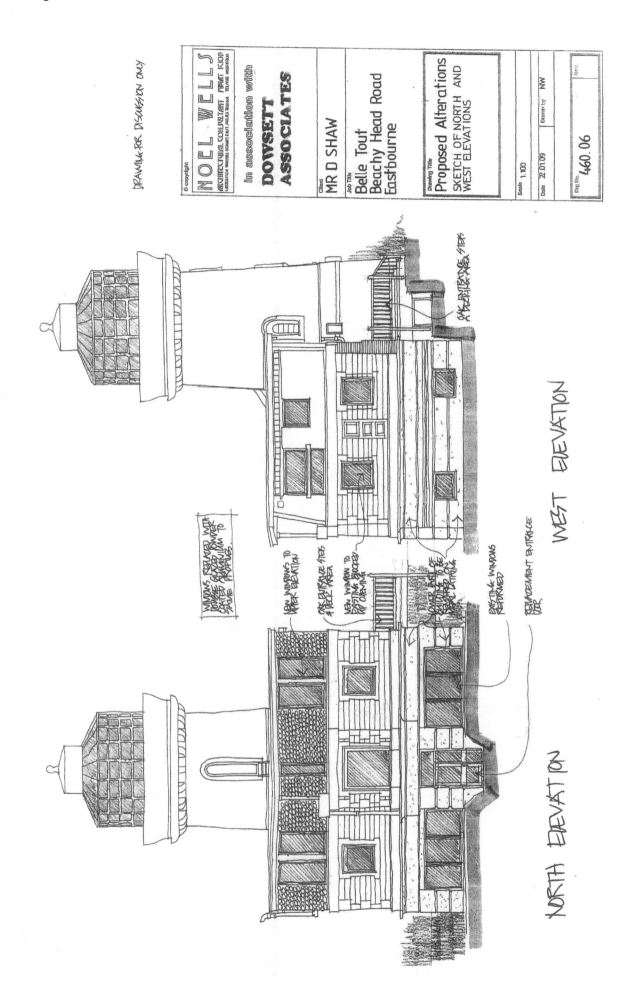

Proposed alterations to Belle Tout, north/west elevations by architect Noel Wells And Dowsett Associates.
(Courtesy of Dowsett Associates)

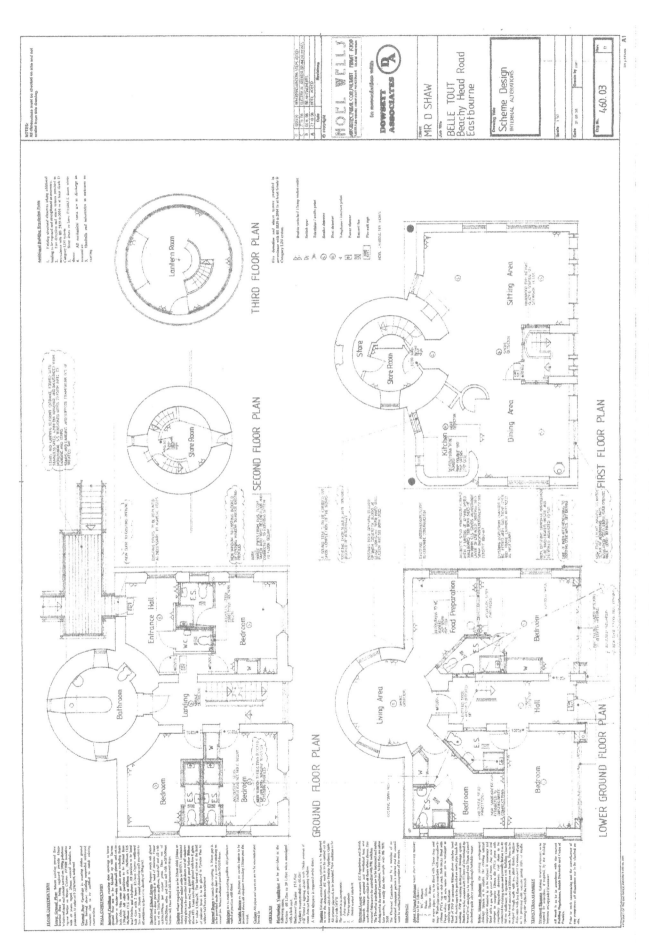

Proposed interior plan for Belle Tout, dated 1.08.08. by architect Noel Wells And Dowsett Associates.
(Courtesy of Dowsett Associates.)

Belle Tout being undertaken. The 1999 move had allowed a longer lease of life of the building, but continuing cliff erosion meant that a further move would be required at some time if the building was not to be lost. Abbey Pynford, the contractors employed to carry out the first move, were contacted as the supporting beams used in the first move were still in place and could be accessed on the lower ground level. This would assist with the considerable cost if a further move was to be considered.

Following instructions from David Shaw, Dowsett Associates in conjunction with Noel Wells, an architectural consultant, who worked closely with them, was instructed to prepare the necessary planning and building regulation drawings to allow the changes necessary to convert Belle Tout into bed and breakfast accommodation. This was an enormous task and involved many hours of sketch design and discussion with the planning office and conservation officer(s) before final approvals were obtained.

The exterior of the building and in particular the fenestration required many negotiations and some small slit-like windows held a particular fascination for everyone. Research showed that they were attributed to Dr Edward Cullinan (or maybe his son) during his period of ownership of Belle Tout. Following negotiations they were retained and added to, with a further window in similar style giving added light to the dining area.

The existing rotting windows in Belle Tout were all double glazed and we were thus able to replace like with like and undertake improvements where possible. On the lower ground floor two large windows, which were not original, were allowed to be replaced with large triple pane windows. This allowed the view across the South Downs to be maximised.

There had been considerable water damage to the interior of the building caused by leaking windows etc. and this needed to be corrected urgently.

The circular viewing area[at the top of the tower] which was exposed to the extreme of the weather conditions, needed attention to prevent deterioration, including work to the exterior railing round the walkway.

Discussions regarding the rendering of the exterior also took some time and were eventually agreed with the exposed area (revealed following the move) being restored in part and the newly constructed area on the lower ground floor (effectively the platform onto which the lighthouse was moved in 1999) being rendered by an agreed method.

The interior of the building was in a very poor state and the challenge here was to restore it to a reasonable state bearing in mind the property was a Listed Building and was also being turned into B&B accommodation to a high standard. Applications for building regulations approval was submitted and after discussion was eventually agreed and the work carried out.

A protracted discussion on the new access road meant that time was running out on the approved planning application; this was due to expire on May 2010. It was therefore decided to start work on the access within the curtilage of Belle Tout so that it could be claimed that the work had been commenced and could then be completed over the downland (which was in the ownership of the Council) when the negotiations were completed with them. This eventually happened and the contractors completed the new access, which ran from Beachy Head Road to Belle Tout in the spring of 2010.

One interesting item came to light was the original metal door which was found in the grounds of the property. Initially, it had been hoped by the Conservation Officer to return it to its original position on the north elevation of Belle Tout, but this opening was now at first-floor level, due to the additional platform added to facilitate the maintenance of the same height after the move – which was a requirement. In addition, the door appeared to have been filled with cement and was thus extremely heavy and impractical to use. It was therefore agreed to retain it as a feature within the curtilage of the property, and it was mounted on a plinth and located near the southern boundary of the site. All in all the work undertaken during the two year period was demanding, but extremely interesting and it was nice to have been part of the restoration of a very iconic building in the South East of England.'

Noel Wells commented: 'I think Belle Tout has turned out well.'

Tim Dowsett/Noel Wells
Consultants to Dowsett Associates
August 2011

THE BUILDERS' CLUB

David Archer and the Builders' Club were employed to do the extensive repair and renovation work:

'I've been doing various projects for Mr. Shaw for about seven years, and he rang me up and asked, 'I've got another project, would you like it?' I

Renovation of Belle Tout tower August 2008.
(Picture by author.)

replied, 'Of course, what is it?' and he replied, 'I've just bought a lighthouse.' I had visions of working somewhere out in the middle of the English Channel, then he told me it was Belle Tout.

I went up to have a look in April 2008 and it was appalling. Rain had been coming in all over the place. There was six inches of water under the floorboards on the lower ground floor and we had to put drains down because it was flooding all the time. The windows were so old and falling apart that water was coming in those. More water was seeping through the actual top of the lighthouse; the rain was coming in through the door and windows there. Where the tower joined onto the main building there was a crack letting in more water. I looked at it all and regarded it as an absolute challenge. It was a building that was listed, had lots of governing bodies overseeing it; it was going to involve a huge amount of work.

We did some initial repair work in June/July 2008 to try to stop the water coming in. We dressed the turret with some lead work, where it had come away from the original building.

The lighthouse was amazingly made. At the top of the tower you had the lantern room and just below the Keeper's Attic, where the lighthouse keeper could lie in bed and keep a check on the light through several glazed holes in the granite ceiling.

Aberdeen granite had been used to build the external walls of the tower, the ground floor and the first floor. Most of the internal walls were brick, which we either exposed and cleaned, or re-plastered.

The Aberdeen granite blocks were all different sizes. We replaced those that were badly damaged with ones we cut to size from surplus granite lying in the grounds. As far as I can tell, when it was hit during the Second World War, the first floor was very badly damaged, but the ground floor remained pretty much OK. A perimeter wall had also been made largely with granite blocks from the site.

The only operating fireplace now is in the lounge. There was a slow combustion stove on the opposite side of the lounge in the present breakfast area. One of the bedrooms in the main building also has a fireplace and there is another in the Keeper's Loft, but neither of these is now operational.

I personally worked on the wooden doors, some dated back to the '50s. It took me two and a half weeks to do twenty-seven doors, including a curved door in the tower, which had to be taken apart to be worked on.

Then there was the arch leading up to the turret; we cleared that and then cleaned off all the old plaster and paint on the inside walls. We then treated all this interior brickwork with a breathable sealant. Metal doors on metal frames, like those in the lantern room, will eventually let water in to a degree but there wasn't a lot more that we could do.

There was a pair of very old metal doors leading up to the tower staircase, which we took off and I renovated. We took out the bunk bed in the top turret room, the Keeper's Attic, which although it looked relatively new, (probably 1950s/'60s) we renovated and put back. In the room below, the Keeper's Loft, there was part of a bunk bed with a cupboard at the back. We renovated and extended the bed into a double loft bed. A shower room was shoehorned in under the stairs as well.

We re-rendered the external walls of the lower ground floor and weatherproofed everything on both levels. I did a lot of the granite renovation myself, re-pointing the granite turret with lime mortar. We then started excavating the car park and there we found lots of WW2 bombs, spent shells and many blocks of stone. I said to the lads, 'We are finding too much granite and sandstone here; what we need to do is make a pile and I'll make something with it at the end.' We had to move a number of the rocks which were so heavy that diggers capable of moving 8 tons couldn't move them. This all went into forming a patio which I called a 'Mini Stonehenge.' In the car park area we made and placed two stone seats.

It is an amazing building that has lasted through so many things. When you are working on a building like that you wonder how much more it can take. I think Mr. Shaw, in the original parts of the building, has spared no expense, because I said to him, 'Look, we're uncovering these things, please let me renovate and restore the fireplaces, the staircase, the sandstone lintels that were over different bits, floors, etc., and he actually let me do that, he didn't have to, and he spent a lot more money, but I think it has been really sympathetically done, to a point where we are really proud of what we have achieved. I now know so much about that building; I've dug up most of the grounds and even found a well near the south-east corner of the building. There is also an old bore hole on the site which I know Mr. Shaw wanted to open up and investigate its potential at some time in the future.

Building Inspector Robin Crowhurst, from Eastbourne Building Control, came along, and working closely with him, we said that we wanted to change this and that, and he was agreeable. He was extremely interested in the lighthouse and found the whole project most fascinating.

We were up against so many things. For example, when we were building the new access road to the lighthouse, the aggravation and grief that we got for doing it, pushed up the cost by over £80,000 more than it should have been. There were further additional costs, too, because of the difficulties experienced getting a substantial electricity transformer across the Downs and onto the site for an upgraded power supply.

Regardless of the problems, I'm really, really pleased with the outcome of the project. We started in 2008 in June, and after a short break we worked right through 2009, finally finishing in the spring of 2010. We must have shifted 500 to 600 tons of chalk from one side of the site to the other. The old road was going from the cliff erosion, and we were still having stuff delivered up there. Natural England said, 'You can't drive on the grass,' to which I replied, 'I'm not letting my lorry drivers go up that road, in 20 and 30 ton vehicles, just 12 inches from the edge of the cliff. I'm not going to do it.'

Working on top of the lighthouse was fun. There was scaffolding there, and we then got ladders to access the very top. This is such a beautiful building. I fitted the new kitchen, because we had to get a square kitchen into a circular room which is quite difficult. Everything had to be cut in, the old worktops were reinforced concrete, and the planners wouldn't let us take them out, so we had to build around them. My brother got a lot of the old Brighton Pier wood, oak, and made the reception desk. Where the bathroom was, with its central bath, we had to leave that in situ, because we weren't permitted to take it out, so we covered it up instead.

This is really a funny story, I was driving to work one day a hot summer's day and it's flooded down at Birling Gap. For about two or three weeks there was more and more water appearing on the road. And early one morning as I was coming to work at 7am I saw water bubbling out from where the bus stop is at Birling Gap. And I thought that this must be a spring. I asked Mr Shaw, 'Is that a spring down there?' and he said, 'No there's no springs down there.' So we phoned Southern Water and they came along and found there was a split pipe and our stopcock was broken. So Mr Shaw had been paying for weeks of flooding at Birling Gap. Usually when you go round someone's house, the stopcock is either under the sink or under the stairs. You don't expect it to be one and a half miles away alongside a bus stop.

Because of the high number of shells that kept turning up, we had a bomb disposal guy permanently on site, plus an archaeologist which cost Mr. Shaw hundreds of pounds a day, every day, for them to stand there. I don't think many of the shells were live, and they took them away, along with fragments of grenades.

We moved the attractive double gates that had been left by the BBC and did a bit of renovation on them. Where they came from was left as a pedestrian track way into Tout's, an ice-cream and tuck shop converted from one of Belle Tout's garages, set into the cliff edge. This is lovely, as people can walk past and see much more of the front of the lighthouse than they could before.

The weather can be really wild up there. When we first started work on the tower we found what we thought were nine bullet holes in the glass. Where they were positioned, there was no way on this planet that someone could have stood out to sea shooting in. This was actually caused by stones being smashed up against the glass by gale force winds.

I lost a couple of windscreens and rear windows in my vans, because some days it gets so windy that it blows all the bits of chalk and stones and it sounds like a horrendous hail shower. It starts off fine, like dust, which can last up to five minutes, and as it gets worse you feel you ought to run and hide.

The snow was a real problem, too, although we did make a couple of nice sledges and sledged down the slope. The rain and the wind – I've never experienced wind that could blow me over.

Something I'd love to know more about is, when the lighthouse was operational, how they mechanically kept the light moving. My thought is that there is a groove cut out of the granite internal wall. When you walk up the staircase, there is a groove running down the inside to the room at the bottom of the turret, and I think a chain went up and down.

I'm extremely happy with what we have done with Belle Tout, finding and opening up many of the original features.'

An interesting diversion for the builders working on the conversion was taking part in the production of the Belle Tout Builder Boys calendar. This was sold in aid of the Everyman charity to 'stamp out male cancer' (www.everyman-campaign.org). The words 'cheeky but tasteful' could be used to describe these novel models, cheerfully posing in the nude around the lighthouse with strategically placed equipment.

Businessman Rob Wassell took the pictures and designed the calendar.

The Belle Tout Builder Boys   2010

Would like to say a big THANK YOU to everyone who made this calendar possible

David and Barbara Shaw
The Belle Tout Lighthouse
www.belletout.co.uk

The Builders Club
For all your building requirements
www.thebuildersclub.co.uk

Rob Wassell
Photograpy & Design
www.rwassell.com

Tansleys Printers
High quality lithographic and digital printers
www.tansleysprinters.co.uk

The **collaborative** project

Enter the 'SPOT THE BUILDER' competition for your chance to win a weekend stay for two at the amazing Belle Tout. Closing date is the 31st December 2009.

www.thecollaborativeproject.co.uk

In aid of

All profits go to charity
www.everyman-campaign.org

Belle Tout Builders Boys Charity Calendar.
(Courtesy of Rob Wassell.)

Advertisement for the Builders Club featuring Belle Tout.
(Courtesy – The Builders Club)

The bathroom at Belle Tout.
(Picture by Bob Fountain.)

The re-designed bathroom.
The old cast iron bath has been boxed in.
(Picture courtesy of John Ball –Building Design)

COMPLETING THE NEW ACCESS ROAD.

Renovation work took around a year, but owing to a long-standing dispute with the council over the inflated cost of the easement (right of way) for the new road, the business had to be put on hold. Planning permission had been granted for the B&B, providing the old access road (now dangerously near the cliff edge) was no longer used by the visiting public. A new road had to be built at the expense of Belle Tout's owners, but this was across council-owned land. Paperwork shown to David Shaw by the previous owners indicated that payment for the easement would be £15,000. However, after he had purchased the lighthouse the council increased the fee to £85,000!

Over more than a year David Shaw negotiated, with accompanying legal costs, to have this reduced to £15,000 again. Eventually the fee was agreed at £40,000. He said:

'I am frustrated and I think this is ironic because this new access road is a requirement laid down by the council. Not only is it costing me to build the road but I now have to pay this grossly inflated easement too. Having seen the paperwork, I believed before I bought the property that the fee payable had been agreed at £15,000. Surely the council is not suggesting this figure was a special rate for the previous owner, Louise Roberts, wife of ex-councillor Mark Roberts. Seemingly another 'generous' deal, like the ludicrously low £900 paid by the Roberts' for the purchase of the freehold a few years ago.'

Barbara Shaw added,
'If people cannot access Belle Tout, our dreams have gone out of the window. We cannot open the lighthouse until we have a new road, and planning permission is running out. We might have to use all of our savings and sell our house. It is very worrying.'

In reply, a council spokesperson said:
'Mr Shaw has requested that the council provides rights over an area of land at Belle Tout, comprising approximately 850 square metres, which will dissect the council's land holding.

The council is under a statutory duty to achieve best consideration for all of its assets. For Mr Shaw the right would provide his property with documented secure access as opposed to the temporary access that currently exists and it is considered that the new access right will substantially increase the value of Belle Tout, whilst the value of the council's holding will decrease.

As regards any earlier offers the council may have made to other parties, like all property transactions, these are without prejudice and subject to contract.'

David Shaw replied,
'I do not agree with all those claims made by the council. This road issue is turning into our worst nightmare. The sticking point is how much more money the council wants. If people can't access the lighthouse, a lot of time and money has been wasted and our dream is gone. We have to have that road.'

However, in February 2010 the problem was finally resolved. Henry Branson, Head of Infrastructure at the council, issued a statement to say that although the previous owners had entered into previous talks with the council in 2003, the matter was not concluded before the property had been transferred to the current owner: 'A deal has been struck so £15,000 is payable by the Belle Tout owners on the signing of the agreement, and a balance of £25,000 will have to be paid upon the next ownership transfer of the Belle Tout.'

New access road. Just started.
(Picture by Mike Smith)

On the website of the American *Lighthouse News* 'Gary' comments, 'The rapacious attitude of city governments, councils, or whatever they are in whichever country they're located in, when it comes to profiting off the world's maritime heritage is disgusting. With property values declining, the value of easement goes up? Why, so that the council can offset other financial losses at the expense of someone else?'

But there were further problems with the road. Because the area is enclosed by a site of a Bronze Age settlement, the road would have to cross over the outer boundary. This had to be done under the supervision of South East Archaeology to make sure that no buried artefacts were damaged. Thus the new road had to be made in a dog-leg shape to accommodate the buried settlement walls, which can be easily seen from the tower as a large, partial ring of dark coloured grass. Half of

New access road. Nearly finished.
(Picture by Mike Smith.)

it has gone into the sea.

Despite the compromise reached regarding the cost of the easement, the actual building of the road turned out to be a nightmare. David Shaw said that further thousands of pounds had to be paid to each of a number of authorities. Additionally, 'the Council proved to be pedantic regarding dealing with the materials required and methodology used in building the road. These caused costs for the road building to spiral out of control, ultimately costing far more than it should have done.'

THE ARCHITECTURAL STAINED GLASS DESIGNER

Ruth Fisher BA (Hons) made and supplied the stained glass compass that is in the ceiling of the tower dome. In 2001–3 she did a degree course in Architectural Glass at Swansea Institute of Higher Education. She then won a 10-week scholarship from the Worshipful Company of Painters and Glaziers to go on a glass-related placement. 'I chose Canterbury Cathedral Studios to learn about glass conservation and restoration which had not been covered on the degree course. It was a real privilege to have an insight into one of our greatest cathedrals and see some of the best glass painters in the country, as well as being involved in a working studio. It was here that a friend phoned me to say there was a stained glass studio for sale in Eastbourne's Enterprise Centre. I came along to have a look, saw it was manageable and bought it.'

David Shaw saw one of Ruth's stained glass door panels picturing the cliffs and Belle Tout:

'... He said he would love to have a similar one for the seaward door of the tower. Having made it, he then asked if he could use the picture for his business cards, which was very flattering.

Then he said he wanted to fill a void in the ceiling of the lantern room. Having seen the programme *Changing Rooms*, when it was filmed at the lighthouse, he'd noticed that in the refurbishment, they had painted a compass on the floor.

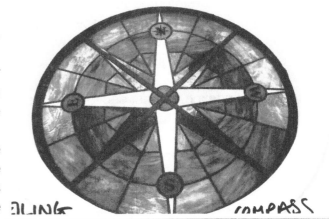

Stained glass compass in roof of the lantern room.
(Picture courtesy of Ruth Fisher.)

I went along with my husband, Simon, who does the fitting for me, so we could have a look. David Shaw had got the measurements of the proposed compass for us, which was 5ft across. So we decided it would have to be made in four pieces, supported by a cross-piece of iron. It couldn't be physically made and fitted in one big piece. I had a look online to see that compass styles would look good in glass and came up with this design. This I left, along with some glass samples, with Mr Shaw and his wife, Barbara, for their approval.

It took a month to make because of the various processes involved. First I had to draw a 'cartoon'; then cut the glass to size; lead up each section, fitting the glass into the lead strips; solder it all; cement one side and wait for it to harden; turn over and solder and cement side two; finally give it a good polish. The glass, much of it iridescent, I bought in sheets from a company in London, and I cut them all to size. I chose this type of glass because it would show up during the day, the light would bounce back off it and the colours compliment the upholstery in the lantern room. The lead, which came from Germany, was in 7ft lengths and various widths. We had lengthy discussions with 'Pete the Steel' about how the steel he was providing should be placed. The strips were quite thin, so there wasn't any room for error, otherwise the glass would have just dropped out. This was

Stained glass front door panel.
(Picture courtesy of Ruth Fisher)

a feat of engineering in itself.

The NSEW letters were contained in special French-made glass discs. In their original state they are clear underneath, covered in a thin layer of cobalt blue. Semantics, a glass engraving business in Grove Road, Eastbourne, masked out the letters, and sandblasted away all the unwanted blue, leaving just the coloured letters set in clear glass. Done this way, they will never come off.

We delivered the finished product one windy day and found a TV company was preparing to film there. We had to weave our way carefully between all the vans and people milling around, it was quite nerve wracking.

Additional complications were caused by attempting to get these fragile sections up the steep and winding stairs to the top of the lighthouse tower. The next challenge was actually fitting the compass.

It is not normal to have leaded panels in a ceiling; they are generally upright in a window, so the compass had to be reinforced inside, to make sure it didn't sag. My husband, who was balanced on the top of a ladder, fitted each piece, and he managed to get three sections dropped in onto the steel cross quite easily. Problems came with the last one, as its outer edge needed to be rested on a small supportive ledge, just where the ladder had been placed.'

After some juggling the last section dropped in:

'I stood underneath watching and praying that it would all fit and my husband didn't fall off. When it was all up there, I heaved a sigh of relief, a big one, and we went home and cracked open a bottle of wine.

I watched the TV programme *Build a New Life in the Country*, which they had been filming when we delivered the compass, saw it featured and thought, 'Now I've made it.' It was such a privilege to make something for a building that is so iconic. I've left my mark on history, the incredible story of Belle Tout. I do think that compass is a nice addition and I'm really proud of it.'

WESTGATE JOINERY'S WINDOWS

After discussing the project with a number of companies and also carrying out extensive research on the internet, Mr Shaw decided that Sussex joinery and timber window manufacturer Westgate Joinery should have the job of replacing the lighthouse's windows, using the revolutionary timber species Accoyao.

Westgate Joinery stated:

Building owners and designers have an increasing number of factors to take into account when considering which materials to specify for use in window fabrication within their buildings. These factors include durability and life expectancy, air and weather tightness, stability throughout changing seasons, energy efficiency, future maintenance cycles and both initial and whole life costs. In addition, sustainability and the impact on the environment of materials chosen is increasingly at the forefront of the decision making progress.

These decisions became even more critical in exposed and coastal locations and this was evident to David Shaw when he purchased the iconic 177-year-old Belle Tout lighthouse perched on the cliffs above the sea at Beachy Head, Eastbourne, Sussex, in 2008 and set about an extensive renovation programme to convert this historic building into an exclusive and very unique guest house.

With the exception of the metal windows around the top of the tower, enclosing the area where the light was once housed, the remaining existing windows were of timber construction in a mixture of styles and timber species and were generally in very poor condition, letting in both wind and rain; they were also inefficient in terms of energy conservation, being, in the main, single glazed.

Following on from discussions with the Local Authority planning and conservation department Mr Shaw made the decision to replace all the windows and set about obtaining advice and quotes for suitable replacements. Bearing in mind the age and location of the building the local conservation officer expressed a preference that the replacement windows should be constructed in timber if at all possible and whilst Mr Shaw in principle was happy to go along with this preference, he was keen to ensure that if possible the manufacturer was UK-based and ideally local to Sussex; he also insisted that the following main criteria were adhered to by this final choice of window manufacturer...

The windows should be of proven design, air and watertight.

As energy efficient as possible.

Require limited ongoing maintenance.

Be cost effective both in terms of initial and whole life cost.

Be manufactured from timber species which are as durable as possible but also from certified sustainable sources.

Have a secure and reliable hinge and locking system.

According to Westgate Joinery's managing director, David Pattenden, Accoyao was an ideal choice for the Belle Tout lighthouse window project:

In addition to the benefits afforded by Accoyao the replacement windows now being installed in this landmark project have the added benefit of high quality stainless steel, or 'tri-coated' multi-point locking systems and 'easy-clean' hinges together with an 'A' rating under the BFRC's Energy Rating scheme demonstrating the energy saving credentials of the product.

Accoyao uses uniform, plantation-grown, sustainable timber, which undergoes a chemical modification process known as acetylation using non-toxic acetic acid to change the cell structure throughout the timber. Invisible to the naked eye, the change creates the most moisture-resistant and durable timber available for joinery and window production. It comes with a minimum service life of 60 years, according to the Building Research Establishment (BRE), which combined with extended maintenance cycles gives significantly lower whole life cost. It also offers class one durability together with exceptional coatings performance and stability through changes in moisture content throughout the climatic seasons.

It is the Gold Standard in wood modifications and is increasingly attracting major interest from architects, specifiers and other manufacturers. The fact that Accoyao demonstrates only negligible changes in sectional dimensions when exposed to variations in moisture content is a major advantage. There is no need to design around movement in the way that solid timber demands. Westgate Joinery has now used the material in numerous diverse and successful projects and Mr Shaw's decision to use Accoyao for the Belle Tout project is yet another vote of confidence in the material.

REDESIGNING THE GROUNDS AND ACCESS

Belle Tout and its boundaries are historically, ecologically and archaeologically valued sites, and protected by many covenants. While excavation and re-designing were undertaken during 2008–10, watching briefs were carried out by various involved bodies, including English Heritage, Archaeology South East, RPS Ordnance, the local authority town planner, the Downland, Trees and Woodland manager, and Natural England. It was the job of John Ball, from Building Design – Chartered Architects, to produce the design, obtain all statutory authorities' approval and pull everyone together before and during the construction stages.

A brief summary of the events that relate to statutory approvals handled by Building Design is as follows:

13 April 2004, Mr and Mrs Roberts: Obtained full planning and listed building consent to add new gates and parking to the rear of the lighthouse and a new access road.

1 April 2009, David Shaw: Submitted a planning application for the approval of details reserved by condition to enable Mr Shaw to start work and to validate the previous approval. Most conditions were discharged shortly after the application.

15 May 2009: Scheduled Monument consent from the Department for Culture, Media and Sport.

9 September 2009: Planning application for the re-siting of the electricity transformer approved.

15 January 2010: Amendment to the approval granted in relation to the car park, the roadway and the point of access into the lighthouse site.

31 March 2011: Approval granted for project to date including all external work.

Rare plants grow well in the chalky soil of Beachy Head. As protected species, their survival in the area during excavation was ensured by John Curzon and Neil Irvine of Natural England. Their website states that 'Belle Tout camp, Birling Gap, is in multiple ownership and benefits from various management actions, including an Environmentally Sensitive Area Scheme and scrub and rabbit damage prevention programme. However, it also suffers from severe cliff erosion.' Neil Irvine said that their watching brief oversaw 'any signs of disturbance, making sure it was kept to a minimum, protecting chalk

Exterior renovations.
(Picture courtesy – John Ball – Building Design.)

grassland species'.

Mike Smith, Downland Trees and Woodland manager for Eastbourne Borough Council stated:

'My job as Downland manager was to act on behalf of the landowner, Eastbourne Borough Council, to ensure that any works undertaken on our land did not damage the grassland habitat, which is designated within a Site of Special Scientific Interest, administered by Natural England.

Under the legislation, as landowner, EBC could have been prosecuted had we not involved, discussed and got approval from

Vans and equipment stored in the lay by.
(Picture courtesy of John Ball – Building Design.)

Natural England, and my brief was to ensure that the works approved by our planning department were undertaken as indicated and that any damage to the grassland surrounding the work area was minimised.

As stated above, it was historic chalk grassland that needed to be protected, but there were orchids present around the work site during the construction of the access.

The downland turf from the initial works was carefully lifted, stored, watered and relaid when the drive was completed, and a native grass seed mix was used on the drive. But the seed was not very successful due to the dry weather following the works.

The actual works commenced at the beginning of April and were completed in May, although I have been dealing with the possibility of a new access since 2003.

My assistant Arboricultural officer, Lee Michael, and I visited the site on a daily basis, often twice a day when required, to resolve issues that arose during the works.

I am satisfied that the works comply with the specification submitted in the planning application and pleased with the way the indigenousness turf has taken, but a little disappointed at the seed not taking, which would have helped lessen the visual impact of the drive when viewed from the east.'

The Eastbourne Downland Management five year plan for 2007–12 for the area covering the old Downland and part of the new Downland at Hodcombe (adjacent to the Belle Tout lay-by) are part of the Seaford to Beachy Head site. The document mentions that under traditional management practices there has been an increase in Bee, Pygmy, Early Purple and Early

The re-sited ornate gates left by the BBC after filming the 'Life and Loves of a She-Devil.'
(Picture courtesy of John Ball- Building Design.)

Spider orchids. The archaeology in this area is important, with horizontal banks and ditches from the Beaker period (Bronze Age), and the area within the earthworks is a Scheduled Ancient Monument (SAM), which is an English Heritage-controlled statutory designation.

Jim Stevenson, Jon Sygrave and Daryl Palmer from Archaeology South East undertook a watching brief, which was outlined in their Written Scheme of Investigation: 'The area is considered to have high archaeological potential ... The Belle Tout lighthouse lies within a series of earthwork enclosures which are designated as a Scheduled Ancient Monument ... The inner enclosure, and its now lost companion, through cliff erosion, are thought to date to the Late Neolithic/Early Bronze Age.'

During the exterior alterations to the gardens, car park and road, Archaeology South East kept a watching brief during an unexploded ordnance survey across the location, made a written and photographic record of the ground reduction of the car parking area and associated driveway, and the breaching of a historic flint wall.

Phase 3 – will comprise the ground reduction of the road corridor ... specific care will be taken where the road crosses the line of the exterior enclosure ditch. Phase 4 – will comprise the hand excavation of the bank, including the turf ... A full black and white, and colour photographic record will be maintained ... All finds recovered from excavated deposits will be collected and retained in line with the ASE artefacts collection policy. Any finds of human remains will be left *in situ*, covered and protected. The coroner's office will be informed ... The sampling will aim to recover spatial and temporal information concerning the occupation of the site.

Mark Landymore and Lawrence Millett from RPS Ordnance Nucleus at Dartford, were on hand in case more Second World War shells were unearthed. In an interim report, dated 16 April 2009, Mark Landymore wrote:

During the Explosives Site Safety Supervision, 20 projectiles were recovered. These were all identified as solid shot and were removed from the site that afternoon by the Army. (11th EOD Regt 621 EOD Squadron) having been examined and subject to X-Ray. They were free from explosives ... It would appear that a legacy of WWII munitions is located across this area and that although HE rounds have not been recovered as yet, there remains the risk that UXO will continue to be encountered during intrusive works. RPS considers it would remain prudent that Explosive Site Safety Supervision remains present on this site to supervise proposed future works and those of any archaeological investigations.

Because it was perilously close to the cliff edge, the transformer supplying electricity to the lighthouse was moved from the south side of Belle Tout and placed on the north side adjacent to the entrance steps. Ian Russell of EDF Energy supervised this project.

The proposed site plans drawn up by Building Design list a large range of various other exterior works, including 'a stone retaining wall matching the existing; ground relevelled and turfed in the garden area; use existing stones for laying paving slabs and stone blocks forming two enclosures as a barbeque; rendered wall with stone coping; and designing both the interior and frontage of the Touts refreshment shop which was to be set inside a 'cave' on the seaward side'.

Mark Weston and Graham Kemp, highways engineers for Eastbourne Borough Council, approved the traffic control method statement, and David Archer and his highway contractor supplied the equipment and managed the traffic during the contract to build the new access road and bell-mouth where it joined the A259.

Permission was given by Melanie Thompson, Amenities Manager (Car Parking) for Eastbourne Borough Council, for Portakabins, essential items for major work such as this, to be sited in part of the car park for the duration of the contract.

The old and uninhabited Cornish Farm, owned by Eastbourne Borough Council, which stores machinery there, was used for stacks of rolled-up turf, laid out on black sheeting and kept watered: it had to go back on the downland in exactly the places from which it had come. The contractors rented part of the lay-by car park at the bottom of the old road, screened it off and stored the blocks for the new road there, alongside the stone cutter, diggers and dumper trucks.

Other personnel on site, overseen by a foreman, were labourers, bricklayers, turfers, a machine operator and a truck driver.

John Ball of Building Design said, 'This contract involved many parties who all worked together very well and to programme, with a good quality result in providing a new road and a layout around the lighthouse that is very unusual and sensitively incorporated into the landscape. It was a site that kept you fit, exposed you to the elements, and it has a very positive, ancient presence.'

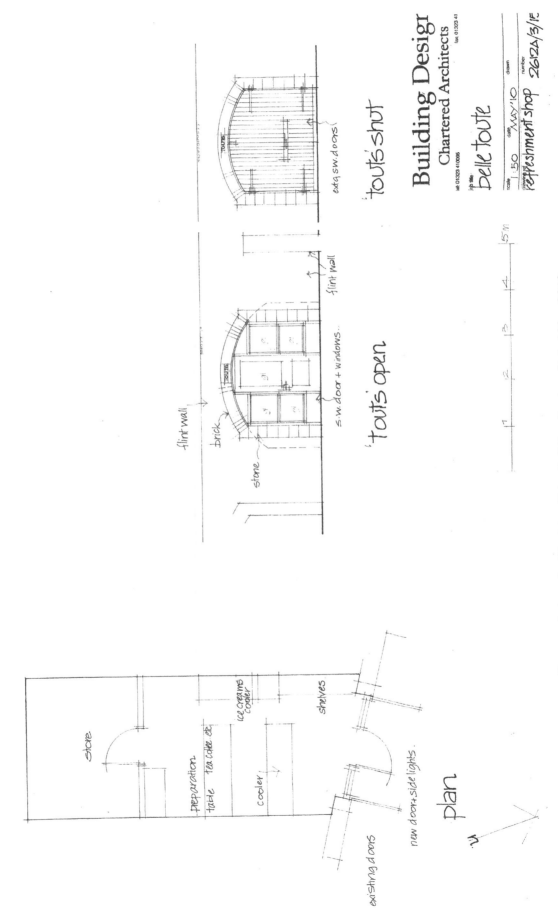

Proposed plans for 'Touts' café by Building Design. Dated May 2010.
(Drawing courtesy of John Ball –Building Design.)

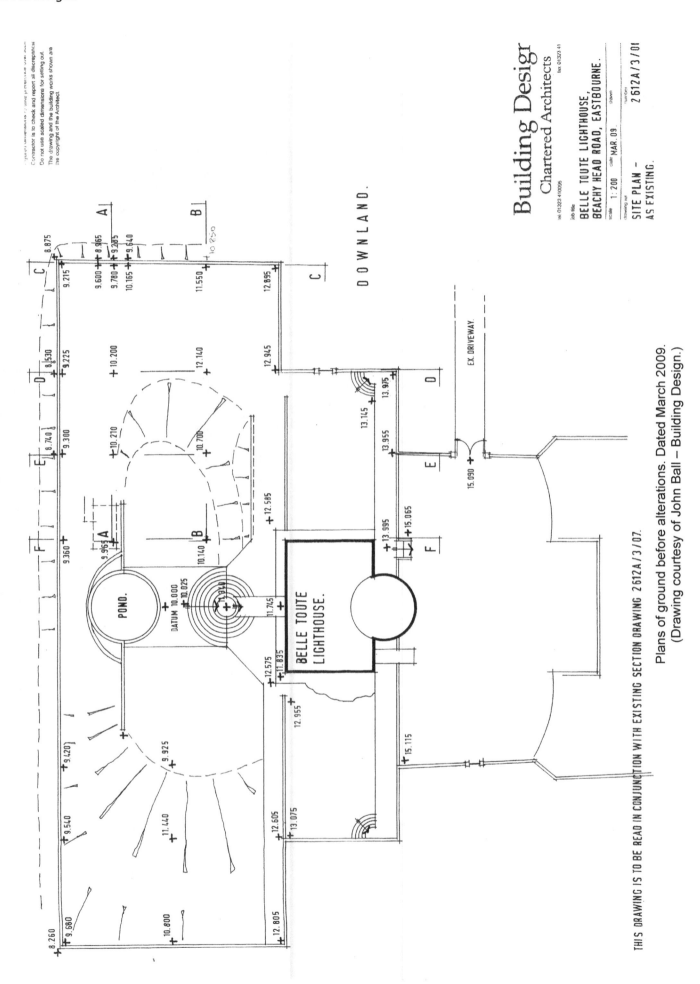

Plans of ground before alterations. Dated March 2009.
(Drawing courtesy of John Ball – Building Design.)

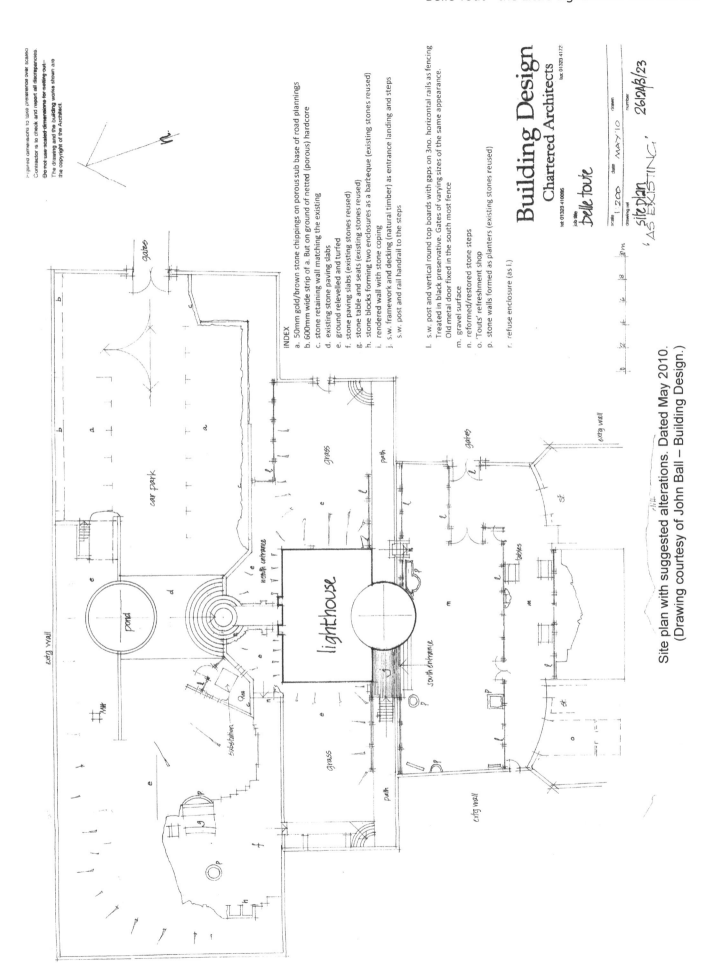

INDEX

a. 50mm gold/brown stone chippings on porous sub base of road plannings
b. 600mm wide strip of a. But on ground of netted (porous) hardcore
c. stone retaining wall matching the existing
d. existing stone paving slabs
e. ground relevelled and turfed
f. stone paving slabs (existing stones reused)
g. stone table and seats (existing stones reused)
h. stone blocks forming two enclosures as a barbeque (existing stones reused)
i. rendered wall with stone coping
j. s.w. framework and decking (natural timber) as entrance landing and steps
k. s.w. post and rail handrail to the steps
l. s.w. post and vertical round top boards with gaps on 3no. horizontal rails as fencing Treated in black preservative. Gates of varying sizes of the same appearance. Old metal door fixed in the south most fence
m. gravel surface
n. reformed/restored stone steps
o. 'Touts' refreshment shop
p. stone walls formed as planters (existing stones reused)
r. refuse enclosure (as l.)

Building Design
Chartered Architects
tel 01323 410095   fax 01323 4172.

job title *Belle Tout*

scale 1:200   date MAY'10   drawn

Drawing ref   number

Site plan 'AS EXISTING',   26/24/3/23

Site plan with suggested alterations. Dated May 2010.
(Drawing courtesy of John Ball – Building Design.)

Figured dimensions to take preference over scaling
Contractor is to check and report all discrepancies.
Do not use scaled dimensions for setting out.
The drawing and the building works shown are
the copyright of the Architect.

129

THE B&B

It was a scramble to get Belle Tout ready for guests. The first bookings had to be cancelled because the access road was not finished. David Shaw and Barbara launched the opening of their luxury bed and breakfast business on 11 May 2010 with a celebratory black tie cocktail party. Invited were the residents of East Dean and Friston. Groups of guests were given guided tours of the newly refurbished accommodation and the lantern room at the top of the tower, from where they watched a glorious sunset. Peter Hobbs, chairman of the Village Hall fundraising committee, presented a bouquet of flowers to Barbara and a bottle of B&B, Benedictine and brandy, to David.

The original managers, Paul Maltby and Nigel Rudd, offered guests a warm welcome, and there was the luxury of a glass or two of wine in the lantern room, where guests could sit and watch ships go by and the sun go down.

In the grounds, and open for each summer season is a tea-shop, 'Tout's,' run by the Shaws' son, Simon, where visitors and walkers on the South Downs Way can refresh themselves with a welcome cup of tea, coffee or an iced drink.

In July Fiona Sturges, writing for the *Independent*, stayed the night at Belle Tout: 'The spectacular restoration of this once imperilled cylinder of limestone and concrete has resulted not only in a proud local landmark but a luxurious space for guests to unwind without squandering the features that make it so unique.' She pointed out that the lamp room at the top of the tower had been newly upholstered and there was a telescope provided 'through which you can spy on passing ships'. Each room had a theme: the Beach Hut has grey-blue hues; the Old England is 'decorated with warm woods, fringed lamps and a cast-iron bedstead.' All were en-suite.

Belle Tout is listed in www.tripadvisor.co.uk [June 2013] as being No. 1 in the Eastbourne B&B/ Inns category; No.2 in the South-East of England, and for 2012 and 2013 been awarded the Trip Advisor Certificate of Excellence. One hundred and forty-four testimonials on that website were highly complimentary, as were the comments from departing guests:-

This place is amazing! Everything is absolutely top notch. Mr and Mrs. Shaw have found absolute treasurers in Nigel and Paul. Nothing, I repeat, nothing is too much trouble for them ... We stayed in the Beach Hut themed room, surely the most luxurious.

The perfect seaside retreat.

A truly magical place.

Wow, what a fantastic experience, unforgettable and definitely to be repeated. I'm a fairly experienced traveller but this lovely unique building took my breath away.

We were met upon our arrival by Paul who after showing us our rooms immediately offered us tea/coffee/cakes/biscuits ... the whole place is remarkable, our room was spotlessly clean with pillow cases ironed by hand ...

Best independent hotel/B&B we have stayed at. First class rooms, delicious breakfast. Owners and managers top notch. Will go back.

Everything about this hotel is perfect in every way, the guys who are the managers, the food they put in front of you every morning, their hospitality, the wonderful and unique rooms, the lamp room, the views, the locations, the fantastic restoration of such a unique building. The term bed and

Belle Tout
Lighthouse

Beachy Head • East Sussex

Unique Bed and Breakfast

As featured on TV's
'Build a new life in the country'

Photographs courtesy of Rob Wassell. Leaflet designed by Sue Rudd.

Belle Tout
Lighthouse

Unique Bed and Breakfast

A few quotes from the many testimonials we have been delighted to receive either directly or through www.tripadviser.co.uk.

"outstanding location with stunning views"
"we loved it and plan to be back soon"
"a truly amazing experience, we didn't want to leave"
"worth every penny – inspirational"
"totally entranced – a great time, a lovely place"
"a wonderful four days for our anniversary treat"
"what lovely memories – a historic Lighthouse set on a dramatic cliff edge with awesome views"

With en-suite room rates for two people of between approximately £150 and just over £200 per night inclusive of breakfast and VAT, your dreams of actually staying in a lighthouse can be realised. Brilliant and different for celebrating that special occasion.

The Company has a policy of a minimum stay of 2 nights, but one night stays can be booked, up to one week in advance, subject to availability. We regret we are unable to accommodate children under the age of 15 or pets.

Please see full details and prices on www.belletout.co.uk and phone to check availability and inclusive price for the dates you would like to book.

Belle Tout Lighthouse, Beachy Head, Eastbourne, East Sussex. BN20 0AE.
Tel: 01323 423185
Email: info@belletout.co.uk
www.belletout.co.uk

Welcome to

Unique Bed and Breakfast

Campaigning from as early as 1691 for a lighthouse on this ancient Neolithic settlement headland, resulted in Belle Tout being built in 1832/34. After almost 70 years life saving service, it was decommissioned in 1902 and Beachy Head Lighthouse, down on the shoreline, took over. Belle Tout became mainly a private residence and in 1935 King George V and Queen Mary were guests, being friends of Sir James Purves-Stewart, the then owner.

Belle Tout Lighthouse survived the 1939/45 war despite being extensively damaged by friendly fire! In the 1950's it was lovingly restored by Dr Edward Revill Cullinan and the present day design of the living quarters contain iconic features that are examples of the earliest work of his son, now eminent architect Edward Cullinan. The mid 1980's saw it owned by the BBC and used by them for filming 'The Life and Loves of a She Devil'. Being a film location manager's dream building and setting, Belle Tout has featured in a number of films and TV productions.

In 1999, because of cliff erosion, the lighthouse was moved back 57ft to safely from the 300ft high cliff edge in an amazing engineering feat that received worldwide publicity, substantially increasing the knowledge of Belle Tout as one of the most famous lighthouses in the world.

In a very dilapidated condition, it was bought by its present owners in 2008 and over a 2 year period, renovated and restored to its former glory to provide comfortable accommodation for just a few guests at a time, to experience the thrill of staying in what must be, one of the most unique and historic buildings, set in its stunning location.

Brochure for Belle Tout as a B&B.
Courtesy of David and Barbara Shaw.)

131

Belle Tout has been lovingly
restored and renovated so that
guests can enjoy a comfortable
and memorable stay at
the Lighthouse

SHIRAZ   BEACH HUT   CAPTAIN'S CABIN   OLD ENGLAND

NEW ENGLAND   VIEW FROM KEEPER'S LOFT

Reception floor

SHIRAZ
Warm rich colours reminding guests of sunnier and more exotic climes.
Double aspect with stunning views along the Seven Sisters coastline towards Birling Gap and back over the undulating contours of the Downs.

BEACH HUT
Seaside colours with a beachside influence transporting guests to beach holidays of yesteryear.
Double aspect with unrivalled coastal views including Beachy Head Lighthouse and the glorious landscape of the Downs.

CAPTAIN'S CABIN
Enjoy being the Captain and his Guest in this cosy cabin. Feature brick wall and original fireplace.
Fabulous sea and Downland views towards Beachy Head and the currently operational lighthouse.

Ground floor

OLD ENGLAND
A slightly larger room, more traditionally furnished, with the benefit of a bath as well as shower ensuite.
The bed faces the wall-to-wall picture windows, giving pastoral views of the beautiful South Downs.

NEW ENGLAND
Similar in size to Old England, but furnished in a modern American style with traditional colours.
Picture windows overlooking the stunning panorama of the South Downs.

Upper floor

KEEPER'S LOFT
The tiny, quirky, original Lighthouse Keeper's own room in the tower itself, with feature brick walls and fireplace. Retained original fixed ladder giving access to the double mezzanine loft bed.
Views along the cliff edge to the east.

All our bedrooms have ensuite shower and wc, tea and coffee making facilities, T.V (with DVD and CD player), hairdryer and a personal safe.

LOUNGE

Relax in comfort in this delightful room. On cold stormy days, warm your toes by the fire. Amazing sea and coastal views and pastoral Downland vistas through the restored 'living picture feature 'Cullinan' windows.

BREAKFAST ROOM

Enjoy your 'Belle Tour' full English or continental breakfast – or both, whilst viewing outstandingly beautiful scenery including the new (1902) Beachy Head lighthouse.

In the Tower

KEEPER'S ATTIC
Climb one flight of stairs to the Keeper's Attic – originally the other Lighthouse Keeper's own room. (Not available as a guest room).

LANTERN ROOM

One more short flight of narrow stone steps takes you to the top of the tower where the Lantern Room affords incredible and unforgettable scenery – 360 degrees of land and seascape views that must rank amongst the best in the world. This is the place to fully appreciate the beautiful and peaceful setting of Belle Tout Lighthouse. Perhaps enjoy a lovely sunset or relaxing music (digital radio with ipod dock and C.D – so bring your ipod and favourite C.Ds). In suitable weather, step out onto the circular walkway surrounding the Lantern Room.

Brochure for Belle Tout as a B&B.
(Courtesy of David and Barbara Shaw.)

David and Barbara Shaw in the lantern room.
(Picture courtesy of Rob Wassell.)

breakfast doesn't do this place any justice whatsoever.

Walking into Belle Tout is like entering the Tardis. It seems impossible to have crammed so much into what appears from the outside to be a not very large building. But David and Barbara Shaw have achieved it. The interior is light, bright and clean. The lounge, with comfortable furniture, abuts the breakfast area, where guests can eat their meals looking out of a large picture window at the wonderful views of Beachy Head and the red and white striped lighthouse. 'This window,' David said, 'once had a frame that was so rotten there were chunks falling off it. The previous owners, Mark and Louis Roberts, had stuffed old clothes into the holes to try and stop the draughts blowing in. Louise and her four children appeared to be almost camping out in the liveable areas of the lighthouse, away from the damp and seeping water. The heating was kept turned up high and every time we visited, it always appeared cosy in there.'

In the corner of the lounge area there stands an old grandfather clock. 'I bought that at an antique fair being held at Ardingly Show Ground. The reason – if you look at the top right-hand corner you will see there is a lighthouse painted there, and it's not unlike Belle Tout.'

Pictures adorn many of the walls, many associated with the building: Dennis Waterman and Patricia Hodge cuddling together on the balcony, taken when they were starring in *The Life and Loves of a She-Devil*; a print of the original lamps flanked by two lighthouse keepers; a large map showing hundreds of shipwrecks around the nearby coastline.

The original bathroom has been converted into a laundry room, but the central cast-iron bath is still there. It is boarded up, although there is a little access door so items can be stored in it.

Workmen pulling off peeling plaster discovered a brick archway where the building abuts the tower at the base of the stairs. Years of neglect and water intrusion had caused an enormous amount of destruction. 'A workman coming to look at this quickly stepped backwards and commented that this problem must be sorted out right away, or we might find bricks around our ears. Now we have a RSJ [rolled steel joist] holding it all up.' Here it was that King George V stood and rebuffed Queen Mary's comments before making an arduous climb to the lantern room. 'Perhaps we ought to put a plaque here saying something to the effect that you are standing right where the king stood.'

Part way up the stairs there is a discoloured patch of brickwork on the seaward side, adjacent to one of the little windows. Apparently this is a patch of repair work that filled in a large hole caused by one of the shells fired from the adjacent gunnery range. Not only did it smash through the brickwork, but it ended up pushing one of the granite blocks out of its bed on the seaward side: this projecting piece of stonework can still be seen on the outside today. 'As this is part of Belle Tout's history, we have to leave the patching just as it is.'

The lantern room has been overhauled, as 'it used to let in a torrent of water when it rained, and there was a waterfall running down the stairs. Cleaning the windows set a challenge. We asked a couple of companies to come and have a look, but they only came the once and we never saw them again. The rain does a lot of this work for us; otherwise we open the windows at the top and pour jugs of water down the glass.'

David and Barbara Shaw had an idea even before the builders had finished about how the rooms might be decorated:

'We wanted a theme within a theme; we didn't want Belle Tout to be like a Disney hotel with outrageous aspects. We decided to name each room, and then during the next two years, as we were out and about, we collected together the furniture and items we needed, where and when we saw them. The name Shiraz came from a wine appreciation tasting event in East Dean village and I thought this was a lovely name for a room, which conjured up warm colours, dark reds that look like wine. It gives an appearance of not looking too British. Old England is traditional, not too bright colours; New England is light and bright. Has an American flag, there's stars and stripes. Captain's Cabin, because the room is fairly small, we couldn't agree about the bed that we put in there. We originally felt bunk beds would take up less space so it looked like a captain's cabin on a ship, but it didn't quite work. There was more room with bunk beds in there but we ended up putting in a proper bed. And to theme it we put in bits we had collected from our cruises, including an original letter from the commodore of one of the cruise ships. We had a block off one ship, and at the Ideal Homes Exhibition we found a stand selling furniture that looked like sailing trunks, so we bought a bedside table and also a matching dressing table-cum-desk. In that room originally we had a director's chair that looked the part, a nautical table lamp and a model of a ship.'

Next door is the Beach Hut. The idea of the décor came from a recently renovated flat that the Shaws own in Seaford. 'I really loved the colours that we had in this flat, it felt like being in a beach hut. All the bits came along with that theme. The pine furniture was distressed. We had ice creamy colours and stripes and the bunting around the room as if you were by the seaside.'

The Keeper's Loft, the lower room in the tower, wasn't being used when the Roberts' had the lighthouse. Originally there was a fixed single bunk and a boiler; 'it was basically a glorified storage space.' Now it has a fixed ladder that goes up to a double mezzanine loft bed. The shower room that has been added was built into an area once occupied by a large understairs cupboard.

Above is the Keeper's Attic, which is not a guest room but spare accommodation 'if any of the staff are deputising and might need to stay overnight. Previously one of the original managers used it as a treatment room, for massage, but that never really worked out.'

David continues:
'The kitchen stayed where it was, but was thoroughly renovated. The company Howdens wanted to be associated with the lighthouse project and the publicity that went with the filming of *Build a New Life in the Country*. They generously donated the kitchen and the fittings, the whole thing, and that included the kitchen in the manager's flat, too. They also added a range cooker and American fridge freezer. Howdens

Renovating the kitchen.
(Picture courtesy of John Ball – Building Designs.)

said, 'Come and take what you want.' Builder David Archer had to customise it and he made a brilliant job of it.'

The furniture for the lounge area was collected and stored at the Shaws' house. 'It was no exaggeration to say that one of our rooms was so full of furnishings we couldn't walk from one end of the room to the other because it was absolutely stacked, plus our double garage was full from floor to ceiling with things we had been buying. We'd see something, like a nice antique chair, various pictures, or sideboards at an antique auction. It was very important that we themed the rooms otherwise we would have bought loads of stuff and wondered where we would eventually put it.'

Renovating the interior of Belle Tout.
(Picture courtesy of John Ball-Building Designs.)

Barbara said, 'I'm a great believer in that if you have some items that are expensive and really nice, you can add other things that are less expensive as long as you are careful. You don't have to spend a fortune, but you definitely need something that adds class.'

David added, 'We didn't stint on the beds, mattresses or bed linen; we spent a lot of money on these. People's tastes on mattresses are so different: some need firm beds, others needs soft mattresses. In Cheltenham we found a local shop selling mattresses that were a combination of spring interior and memory foam. These proved a great success and several of our guests wanted to know where to buy the same.'

Barbara continued:
 'With the choice of fabrics, I felt that although we were having different themes in every room I didn't really want, say, swags and tails in one room and something different, like blinds or voiles, in another, so by unifying every room with roller blinds and having stripes in the fabric of each room in keeping with the theme it ties it all together, and makes it a bit seasidey.

As for the lantern room, everyone said that they expected us to put in ships' wheels, lifebelts and navy blue and white stripes everywhere. I felt that this was so obvious we were not going to do this, choosing instead sea colours, the shades of aquamarine that complement the sea, and not make it look like a ship. The cushions are the same greeny-blue colour. We originally had the idea of putting armchairs in the lantern room, so it might have looked like a gentlemen's club room. But the problem with normal height chairs, people would have been straining their necks to look out of the windows. Then I had the idea of purpose-built chairs on a raised platform and I think it works very well.'

David explains that there is a minimum two nights' stay at the lighthouse:
'You need at least that period of time to fully enjoy the Belle Tout experience. With a checking-in time of 4pm and a departure time of 10.30am, one day is not enough to appreciate all that is on offer. Although, if we have vacancies and any walkers on the South Downs Way ring the doorbell and need a room for just one night, we are happy to oblige. Also, one night stays can be booked within seven days of the date required, obviously subject to availability. There are cotton dressing-gowns available on order when booking, plus bedroom slippers, on request, that guests can take away afterwards.'

Outside, the remnants of the old lighthouse foundations are perched perilously close to the edge of the cliff. David Shaw observed, 'If they hadn't moved the lighthouse, it would still be standing there – just.'

The B&B has been successful from day one, many of the guests having heard about the newly opened business from the popular television programme shown on Channel 5 in January 2010, *Build a New Life in the Country*. The comments from guests have been highly complimentary in general – but there's always one, as David recounted:

'When the wind blows around the cliffs it whips off little pieces of chalk, which we often find lying in some quantity on the surrounding grassland. Children love to pick them up and spell out their names or form hearts on the grass with the bits. We had a phone call from a lady with an educated voice, asking to make a booking. On arrival, she took one look around and told us that she wouldn't be staying with us as there was far too much graffiti!'

Lounge
(Picture courtesy of Rob Wassell.)

Bedroom- The Captain's Cabin
(Picture courtesy of Rob Wassell.)

GHOSTS

As Beachy Head has the reputation of being one of the most haunted places in Britain, it comes as no surprise that Belle Tout has been host to the odd ghostly visitor.

In *Paranormal Eastbourne* author Janet Cameron writes:
There's definitely something about lighthouses that make them ideal venues for a haunting; the isolation, eerily buffeted by the winds and storms, perhaps for many years ... The Belle Tout lighthouse ... is said to be haunted by a lighthouse keeper who hanged himself in the late eighteen hundreds. He continues to haunt the place where he was so unhappy that he decided to end it all. It's easy to see how loneliness, contrasted with the never ending pounding of the waves while living in bleak conditions and very limited space, might drive a man to take his own life.

Builder David Archer had his own story to tell of spiritual visitations:
'When we were doing the inside, we had certain time frames to work to, and because no-one was living there, we occasionally worked up to 12 o'clock at night. There were six of us sitting around the lounge fire one night, having a meal about nine or ten o'clock, and all of a sudden, out of the corner of my eye, I saw this figure dressed all in white run down the stairs. I called out, 'Who's there?' The guys said, 'What do you mean?' I got up calling out, 'Hello, hello,' and the others said, 'What are you doing?' I replied that I'd just seen a figure in white going down the stairs. They just retorted, 'Don't wind us up.' 'I'm not winding you up, I'm telling you now,' and the plastic curtain screening the stairs was flapping. We didn't find anyone.

Another time, I was on the phone to Mr Shaw and going through the specifications. I was on my own with a lamp, there were no electrics, and I was holding my diary and going from room to room. I was standing in the kitchen when I heard a lot of banging like a cupboard door being slammed shut. I called out, 'Hello, hello,' then said, 'Hang on a minute, Mr Shaw, stay on the phone because I think there's someone in here.' So I walked down to the ground floor and then heard this banging coming from the floor above. I thought, 'There's someone here and they're winding me up.' Mr Shaw confirmed this; he too could hear the banging. 'Was it a cat?' he suggested. So I shouted, 'Come out, whoever you are.' I looked out of a window: there were no cars in the car park, and I'd locked the door when I came in and there was definitely nobody about. So there's clearly a ghost there; quite a friendly one, and a little playful. He never gave us any hassle or grief.'

LIGHTS – CAMERA – ACTION

Belle Tout and the surrounding landscape have been a popular choice for many production companies as a film location – not just for the iconic series *The Life and Loves of a She-Devil*. The area offers acres of open South Downs countryside without a pylon or vehicle in sight.

In 1958 the Hammer film company was in the area for *Dick Barton at Bay*. There was a brief glimpse of the downs when Hayley Mills and Deborah Kerr were filming *The Chalk Garden* in 1964. In the children's classic *Chitty Chitty Bang Bang* (1968) the famous car drove off the cliffs, opened its wings and flew.

Quadrophenia, a 1979 film about Mods and Rockers on the south coast, featured a brief background glimpse of the lanternless Belle Tout as disillusioned Mod, Jimmy (Phil Daniels) rides a stolen scooter over Beachy Head cliffs.

Also filmed here were the rock opera *Tommy* (1975) and a TV Agatha Christie film in the Miss Marple series. US TV drama *Still Crazy Like a Fox* was filmed at Belle Tout in 1987. It featured actors Jack Warden and John Rubenstein, who played the part of San Francisco private eyes. During a holiday in England they inadvertently become the prime suspects in a murder and went on the run in the British countryside, with the entire police force on their trail.

A dramatic sequence was filmed here for the James Bond film *Living Daylights* (1987), starring Timothy Dalton. The production company wrecked three Land Rovers to clinch a scene where a secret agent drives over the cliffs and escapes by opening up a parachute. The Beachy Head cliffs were doubling up for the Rock of Gibraltar. A few years later a split-second shot of the beach below Belle Tout featured in *Robin Hood – Prince of Thieves* (1991).

In early 1995, the white cliffs of the Seven Sisters and Belle Tout featured heavily in promotional material to advertise the forthcoming Disney Channel on Sky TV. With computer enhancement the old lighthouse acquired a flashing beam, and Disney characters danced against the white cliffs.

In September 2004 film-makers Warner Bros chose Eastbourne's downland to shoot a section of the popular film *Harry Potter and the Goblet of Fire*. Sue Quinn, the film's location manager, said, 'The setting, close to the sea and the countryside, was perfect for what we were looking for and I think it will look good on film. The location is beautiful, and the climate and weather were perfect today. The filming we are doing ... plays an important part in the film. We'll be using blue screen technology so the actors will be imposed on the background scenery that we are filming here.'

TV commercials have been shot in this area for BMW, Nissan, Vauxhall, Orange, 02, e-on, T Mobile, Phones 4U, Carlsberg, Müller Rice yoghurts and the National Lottery. Laura Ashley has used Belle Tout as a backdrop when filming a commercial to promote more hat sales, and Hank Marvin (from Cliff Richard's Shadows) made a commercial here to promote a disc. Pop videos have been filmed here by Blur, Phil Collins, Sting and Texas.

The end of the well-publicised remake of *Brighton Rock* (2010) was shot here, although digital wizardry turned Belle Tout into a standard lighthouse.

Since 2000 Eastbourne's Film Liaison Unit has been handling most of the interest from film companies that want to use Belle Tout and the surrounding area. It was set up in response to requests for location filming that were coming into the Tourism and Leisure Press Office. Their primary aim is to use film success as a PR and marketing tool for the destination, promoting Eastbourne to new audiences and allowing the town to be seen in media in which the council could not afford to advertise. For example, the success of the film *Angus, Thongs and Perfect Snogging* (2008) showed Eastbourne to a new audience and helped to change the usual perception of Eastbourne. The secondary objective is to generate income for both the council and the destination.

The unit was closely involved with the filming of the remake of *Brighton Rock*, particularly in the Beachy Head area.

Annie Willis, Tourism Development Manager for Eastbourne Borough Council, said:

'Because of the nature of the site, ANOB and SSI status, we had to ensure that tracking was put on the downs for the crane and other vehicles to use, to avoid any damage to the area. There was a massive lighting crane and a rain machine. The unit managed all of the road closures, and for some of the shots 'stop and go' boards were used to stop traffic during the filming. I understand that this is the longest distance that a 'stop and go' board operation has been used. The unit also managed providing stewards, helping provide extras, equipment, accommodation, changing rooms and parking. When filming is done on the Downs we need to get the consent of Natural England, even though the council are the landowners. We delayed the seasonal planting of the carpet gardens [on Eastbourne's seafront] to ensure the set was clear of modern vehicles and gardeners.

During the filming, which took place for three weeks in October 2009, the crews spent £500,000 in Eastbourne and we got significant publicity from the fact that *Brighton Rock* was filmed in Eastbourne – and should be called *Eastbourne Rock*.'

There is a free pocket guide entitled *Lights, Camera, Eastbourne* available from Eastbourne Tourist Information Centre, which sets out all the recent film locations.

Elizabeth Wright

THE MAYOR OF EASTBOURNE'S MEMORIES

Carolyn Heaps was Mayor for Eastbourne in 2011:

'I was invited to view Belle Tout lighthouse by Mr Shaw whom I met at a Motcombe Gardens bowling competition last summer. I gave him a photo that my husband had taken of the lighthouse at sunset which he was very pleased with. We kept in touch and he kindly invited us to the lighthouse to look around one weekend lunchtime, which my husband and I took him up on. We thoroughly enjoyed viewing the fabulous rooms and especially the light tower with its 360 degree views. I asked if I could possibly abseil off the tower for charity at some future date – so who knows, that may occur some time!'

SOUTHDOWN AMATEUR RADIO SOCIETY

The Southdown Amateur Radio Society was formed in June 1967. President Geoffrey Ellis states:

'We frequently establish 'special events' stations at sites of historic or local interest, such as Belle Tout lighthouse, where, with the kind permission of the owners of the day, we have now been for some 20 years. Essentially we exchange radio signal strength reports and greetings in a contest. We use either club amateur radio transmitters, receivers and aerials, or if we are running a multi-station event, members may bring their own equipment for communal use.

We participate in a special International Lighthouses/Lightships on the Air event held annually on the third weekend of August. This is a contest to compete for the greatest number of 'lighthouse to lighthouse' contacts by amateur radio over a two day event.'

Peter Martin, treasurer of the society, added:

'Under Belle Tout's previous owner we had the run of the house and grounds. We operated from the tower rooms after erecting 20 foot masts in the lower garden to support the long wire and G4RV aerials while the UHF and VHF were mounted on the handrail at the top of the tower. A further rhombic was mounted on a pole on the seaward side of the then car park. All modes of transmission were used on most bands depending on the propagation conditions at the time. Being a competition long 'ragchews' [contact between two amateur radio operators] did not happen very often, but a good many worldwide contacts were made, particularly to the USA in the late afternoons. We also erected a large tent on the upper lawn and had a club barbecue for the operators. This format ran for several years until it [Belle Tout] was sold to the present owners; 2010 was the last time we used the site, when we operated from the corner of the new car park.'

The Southdown Amateur Radio Society is twinned with the Rouen based Radio Club de Normandie. By 'the constant exchange of information and ideas, and the fostering of personal relationships, there developed the kind of international friendship for which the radio amateur has become renowned'. Parties of SARS and RCN members visit each other on alternate years.

The International Lighthouse/Lightship Weekend (ILLW), the annual amateur radio weekend event mentioned above, is sponsored by the Ayr Amateur Radio Group in Scotland and is held on the third full weekend in August. This coincides on the Sunday with International Lighthouse Day, an event organised by the International Association of Lighthouse Keepers during which many world lighthouses are open to the public for the day. Four hundred and fifty lighthouses and Lightships in some 50 countries around the world have taken part. Up until 2008, when repairs were under way, Belle Tout was listed as an entrant (UK 003) The purpose of the exercise is 'to promote public awareness of lighthouses ... and their need for preservation and restoration, and at the same time to promote amateur radio and to foster International goodwill. Lighthouses are fast becoming an endangered species with the introduction of Global Positioning Systems and Satellite Navigation and the automation of the light source to solar power, which has resulted in the withdrawal of management personnel (Keepers). It is hoped that this event will highlight this situation and help prevent further desecration of these magnificent structures all around the world.'

A member of the Southdown Amateur Radio Station broadcasting from Belle Tout on a special International Lighthouses/Light ships on the Air event.
(Picture courtesy of Geoffrey Ellis.)

Briony Moorton of Eastbourne's Parkland School with her model of Belle Tout lighthouse.
(Picture courtesy of Sue Smith.)

(1)

My Booklet on Belle Tout Lighthouse

Belle Tout Lighthouse that Moved.

Did you know that Belle Tout Lighthouse
Is completly white and there looks
like there is A little house Bulit
Next to it? Well I can tell you
there is a little house built Next
to it Because the lighthouse
Keeper lives there.
This is A photo of Belle Tout →

Did you know that Belle
Tout has been built for
172 Years But I became
on Sevice On 2nd october
1902. Belle Tout is on
Beachey Head cliffs.

Belle Tout was knocked down
once Before Because It was
Built during world war 2 So that
Is why belle tout was moved and
Built again Because all The gun
shots made holes. So they Nocked
It down and Built it again after
world war 2.

Briony's homework, studying Belle Tout.
(Courtesy of teacher Sue Smith.)

145

THE FUTURE

What does the future hold for Belle Tout lighthouse? As long as there are no serious cliff falls it should take about 30 years before erosion dictates that the lighthouse is moved again. As the underpinning beams from the previous move are still in situ, this should be relatively easy. But there is only about 55ft of spare land left on the north side before a steep slope that plummets down to the road. David Shaw said, 'When I've caught my breath I'll move it again, and to compensate for the drop we'll have to put in two extra floors, although we'll lose one floor when it's moved off its 1999 platform. We might even move it a bit diagonally. I always wondered why the Roberts didn't move it right back the last time.'

Barbara added, 'it will take a lot of organising: there's the planning and the council, it would be horrendous getting all the permits. I'd be happy to leave things for a few years. It doesn't have to be done right now, but David wants to finish the story. He's not ready to retire yet. Certainly within our son's lifetime it will have to be moved again. But we are happy to carry on with it as a B&B.'

Belle Tout hasn't gone unnoticed by a younger generation. At Parkland School, Hampden Park, Eastbourne, helped by teacher Sue Smith, the children of class 4SW have been enthusiastically gathering information about shipwrecks and the work of lighthouses, especially the local Belle Tout. They have built individual models from toilet rolls, cardboard and plastic cups, and added working lights. They have written about their value over the years as working lighthouses and their benefits to shipping.

But as lighthouses become less essential to navigation, many of these historical structures are facing demolition or neglect. Modern navigation is mostly reliant on GPS, feeding data to electronic chart systems to display obstacles, cliff edges, depths, rocks at sea and the position of the vessel.

But GPS systems are not infallible: seasonal sunspot activity can wreck havoc with their data handling, and there is always the threat of terrorist destruction to the satellites. Thus the old ways might still be needed. Time will tell.

Belle Tout, however, has an assured future. David Shaw said, 'I feel very privileged to be part of Belle Tout's amazing history. It is nice to do something different in life, something to be remembered by.'

ACKNOWLEDGEMENTS

My grateful thanks go to the following people, businesses and companies, who provided me with valuable information, facts, anecdotes, stories, recollections and fascinating memories relating to Beachy Head's Belle Tout lighthouse. And special thanks to Gareth Thomas, Eastbourne, for all his technical help in the preparation of this book.

Aberdeen City Archives.
Abbey Pynford Foundation Systems Ltd.
Aberdeen Art Gallery and Museums.
Aberdeen University. (Historic Collections).
David Archer (The Builders' Club).
John Ball – Building Design.
Luke Barber – Research Officer, Sussex Archaeological Society.
Owen Boydell-Eastbourne Society.
Wendy Bishop.
John Boyle.
Julian Bell – Weald and Downland Open Air Museum.
Chas Bell.
Luke Barber – Sussex Archaeological Society)
Ruth Briggs. (Ruth Fisher, BA Hons)
Jenny Brown – Curator, Aberdeen Maritime Museum.
Cranes Today magazine – Will North.
Roz Cullinan.
Ted Cullinan.
Dominic Cullinan.
Mick and Sue Compton.
Maureen Copping – Eastbourne Local History Society.
Dr Oliver Douglas – Assistant Curator of Museum of English Rural Life.
Tim Dowsett- Dowsett Associates.
Eastbourne Local History Society.
Sue Enoch.
English Heritage.
East Sussex Records Office.
Josephine Egger – Switzerland.
Dorothy Forsyth.
Bob Fountain.
Philip Bye (Senior Archivist – East Sussex Records Office.)
Don and Jane Granger – USA.
Councillor Caroline Heaps (Mayor of Eastbourne.)
Sue Houlihan (née Cullinan).
Samantha Hide (East Sussex Library and Information Services.)
Neil Jones – Trinity House Archives.
Tom Lynn.
Derek Legg.
Stephen Lloyd – MP for Eastbourne and Willingdon.
London Metropolitan Archives.
Peter Longstaff-Tyrrell.

The staff from Hailsham, Langney, Hampden Park and Eastbourne Libraries, especially Sue Bartlett, Library Manager at Langney.

Jim Murray.

The Museum of Scottish Lighthouses in Fraserborough.

Julian Martyr.

Peter Martin (Southdown Amateur Radio).

Jane Nesbit – Head, Military History Research Centre, Canadian War Museum.

National Maritime Museum.

Newhaven Maritime Museum.

Melanie McKinnon – Crown Copyright and Licensing (Canada)

Michael Ockenden.

Harry Pope.

M. Plowright.

Parkland School, Eastbourne: Sue Smith and pupils of class 4SW.

Michael Partridge – Eastbourne Local History Society.

Roy Peacock.

Mike Peach.

Pam Rollison.

Richard Rager- Rager and Roberts- Estate Agents.

Graham Robertson – MD of A. &J. Robertson (Granite) Ltd, Aberdeen.

David Renno – author.

Jill Rutherford and friends Naoko Yoshida and Sawako Gomi.

Garry Russell, BEM – retired coastguard.

John Sheppard.

Mark Sawyer (Coxswain Eastbourne Lifeboat).

Mike Smith (Downland, Trees and Woodland Manager).

David and Barbara Shaw – owners of Belle Tout.

Southdown Amateur Radio Society – Peter Martin and Geoff Ellis.

Staff at the copy counter of Eastbourne's Staples.

Trinity House.

Graham Thompson – Eastbourne Rambling Club.

David Viner.

Lys Wyness – Aberdeen Town and County History Society.

Edith Wemyss – Aberdeen Local Studies Library.

Noel Wells – Dowsett Associates.

Westgate Joinery.

David Wells.

Rob Wassell.

Margaret White.

The author – Elizabeth Wright at Belle Tout Lighthouse.

Good bye – Belle Tout.
(Picture courtesy of Mike Smith.)

BIBLIOGRAPHY

Ryan, Sheila, *Untold Stories of Beachy Head* (SB Publications, 2010)

Surtees, John, *Beachy Head* (SB Publications, 1997)

Renno, David, *Beachy Head. Shipwrecks of the 19th century* (Amherst Publishing, 2004)

Woodford, Cecile, *Portrait of Sussex* (Robert Hale, 1972)

Johnson, W.H., *Sussex Disasters* (SB Publications)

Drewett, P.L., 'A section through the Iron-Age Promontory fort at Belle Tout', *Sussex Archaeological Collection*, vol. 113, p.184 (1975)

Ankers, Arthur R., *Sussex Cavalcade* (Pond View Books, 1992)

Moore, Judy, *Silly Sussex* (SB Publications, 2004)

Marsden, Peter, *The History of Shipwrecks of South-East England* (Jarrold, 1987)

Jeese, R.H.B., *A Survey of the Agriculture of Sussex* (Royal Agricultural Society of England, 1960)

Morris, Jeff and Hendy, David, *The Story of the Eastbourne Lifeboats* (Lifeboat Enthusiasts Society, 1988)

Larkin, Monty, *Seven Sisters – The History Behind the View* (Ulmus Books, 2008)

Boyle, Martin, *Beachy Head – lighthouses of England and Wales* (B & T Publishers, 1999)

Beckett, Arthur, *The Spirit of the Downs* (Methuen, 1930)

Hutchinson, Geoff, *Fuller of Sussex: A Georgian Squire* (revised 1997)

Sussex County Magazine

Chapman, Brigid, *Royal Visitors to Sussex* (CGB Cliffe, 1991)

Eastbourne Herald.

Eastbourne Gazette.

Daily Mail.

Makin, W.J., *The Life of King George V* (George Newnes, 1936)

Daily Telegraph

Brighton Argus

Camden New Journal

Lightning Source UK Ltd.
Milton Keynes UK
UKOW07n1400120515

251351UK00009B/91/P